WALKS THROUGH LOST PARIS

LEONARD PITT

WALKS THROUGH LOST PARIS

A JOURNEY INTO THE HEART
OF HISTORIC PARIS

COUNTERPOINT

BERKELEY

To my mother and to the memory of my father. They gave their all.

Copyright © 2006 Leonard Pitt

First Shoemaker & Hoard edition 2006
French edition published in 2002 by Editions Parigramme

Library of Congress Cataloging-in-Publication Data
Pitt, Leonard.
Walks through lost Paris : a journey into the heart of historic Paris / Leonard Pitt.
p. cm.
ISBN-13: 978-1-59376-103-5
ISBN-10: 1-59376-103-1
1. Walking—France—Paris—Guidebooks. 2. Paris (France)—History. 3. City planning—France—Paris—History. 4. Haussmann, Georges Eugène, baron, 1809-1891. I. Title.
DC708.P57 2006
711'.40944361—dc22
2005033896

Designed by Gerilyn Attebery & Megan Cooney
Map on page 11 by Mike Morgenfeld
Cartography by Bénédicte Loisel
Printed in the China through Colorcraft Ltd., Hong Kong

Front cover photo: © BHVP
Back cover photos, from left to right: © BHVP; author's personal collection; © PMVP / Negative offre; © ND–Viollet

COUNTERPOINT
2117 Fourth Street
Suite D
Berkeley, CA 94710
www.counterpointpress.com

Distributed by Publishers Group West

10 9 8 7 6 5 4 3

CONTENTS

Rue de la Masure looking towards the Seine from Rue de l'Hôtel de Ville. Demolished in 1941.

Preface

"How strange it is, this city of ours. We must walk its streets with the soul of an archeologist, like an inhabitant of Pompeii walking among the ruins wondering if he is not being tossed about in a dream." These words of Daniel Halévy, from his book *Parisian Landscapes (Pays Parisiens)*, 1932, could have been written for this book. For the pages that follow are like a large sepia-toned album of lost Paris that guides readers on a voyage through time, plunging them into a nostalgia whose guardian spirits are photographers Charles Marville, Pierre Emonds, Henri Godefroy, Eugène Atget.

But this nostalgia is more than a simple indulgence in the past, for Leonard Pitt knows old Paris beautifully. He does more than simply line up old photos of the city like an arrangement of fruit on a stand. He explains; he pinpoints; he dismantles and compares. More importantly, he lays the images of old Paris over the modern city, revealing the depth of the Parisian past to the attentive stroller. Anyone who suspects that another city stood in its place will see that other city in these pages, in its overwhelming humanity with its lopsided houses, winding streets, wooden shops, and hand-drawn carts.

As if by magic each photo becomes an indictment, a finger pointing at those who "assassinated" Paris, to borrow the vocabulary of sociologist Louis Chevalier. First among them, of course, is Baron Georges-Eugène Haussmann. No need to darken the portrait of this man: Either too admired, or too disliked, the prefect of Napoléon III is not the great man that many have wanted to make of him. As recent research has shown, he was a man of narrow intellect, an efficient administrator devoid of sensitivity. A man who understood nothing of the poetry of the city he treated as though it were a neutral object. A man for whom progress, this "paganism of imbeciles" (Baudelaire), justified so much destruction, so many straight lines and army barracks, demonstrating above all an absence of ideas and a taste for money.

Leonard Pitt does not forget Haussmann's brilliant successors, who, up through Georges Pompidou, wanted to transform Paris into a parking lot, or a freeway dotted with a handful of lodgings. An American citizen *(citoyen)*, Pitt knows Paris, where he studied years ago with the mime Etienne Decroux (whose name is forever linked to the film *Children of Paradise*), so well. His passion; his intimate, at times even staggering, knowledge of old Paris; his energy to search, to understand, to collect old maps, postcards, and engravings, as well as old photos, gives his work an added depth—one could say, a soul. It is not an exaggeration to say that he has earned the recognition, indeed the gratitude, of old Paris. And like historian Alfred Bonnardot a hundred and fifty years ago, he could content himself to sign his work "Leonard Pitt, Parisian."

—ALEXANDRE GADY

Introduction

He who contemplates the depths of Paris is seized with vertigo.
Nothing is more fantastic. Nothing is more tragic.
Nothing is more sublime.

Victor Hugo

THIS BOOK WAS BORN out of ignorance. During the 1960s, while revolution raged on American streets, I lived in a tiny garret on the Avenue de l'Opéra in the heart of Paris. I thought I would stay only a few months, but the city had a hold on me. I stayed for seven years. Coming from the American Midwest, I loved the beauty of this ancient city, and at the drop of a hat would wax poetic at the thought of my centuries-old avenue and the buildings that lined it.

Many years later, long after I had returned to the States, I discovered that the Avenue de l'Opéra and all the buildings on it were barely ninety years old when I lived there. In its place there once stood a rabbit warren of small streets and passageways, a whole other Paris that had been torn down in the mid-19th century. The shock of my ignorance made me wildly curious. I began reading everything I could find about this history, as well as about the man who carried out this rebuilding of Paris: Baron Georges-Eugène Haussmann.

The numbers are staggering. Between 1853 and 1870, Haussmann demolished nearly 20,000 buildings in Paris and constructed 45,000 new buildings. With an army of 60,000 workers laboring day and night, he erased hundreds of streets from the map. Much of the city's history was lost as some of the oldest quarters in Paris, dating back to medieval and Renaissance times, crumbled. The island on which Notre Dame sits, Ile de la Cité, was nearly leveled. The number of Parisians evicted from their lodgings during this urban makeover reached over 100,000. Many of the large avenues and boulevards famous today as symbols of Paris were created during this great urban upheaval.

Returning to Paris to feed my curiosity I spent days in the archives studying old maps, trying to reconstruct the city that existed before Haussmann. I walked through neighborhoods with 19th-century photos in hand, searching for a Paris that no longer existed. I exulted when a photo I had puzzled over for months suddenly fit with the actual street in front of me. My real desire was to get a bucket of paint with a large brush and paint lines on the streets and sidewalks to mark out where the old city ran so everyone could see. My interest grew beyond Haussmann to how the city had changed in earlier centuries, as well as how it continued evolving into the 20th century.

In time I began leading friends on tours through Paris, describing what stood where and how the city had been put together. Later, I created a lecture with slides tracing this dramatic urban history. This book is the fruit of my continuing desire to communicate to others the richness of the history I discovered for myself.

◄ Rue Glatigny on Ile de la Cité, on the site of today's Hôtel de Ville. (Musée Carnavalet, ©PMVP/Negative Degraces)

NAPOLEON III, EMPEROR OF FRANCE

While Haussmann is the key to understanding modern Paris, the real impetus behind this transformation was Napoléon III, nephew of history's more famous Napoléon who lost the battle at Waterloo. Napoléon III, also known as Louis-Napoléon, became emperor in 1852 after a long, hard climb up the greasiest of poles. Twice he tried to overthrow the government and twice he failed. After his first attempt in 1836, he was exiled to that far-off land, America. After his second attempt in 1840, the French government was less amenable and sentenced him to life in prison at Ham, a medieval castle in the north of France replete with drawbridge and moat.

Even with a life sentence before him, Louis-Napoléon never lost faith in his belief that one day he would rule France. Sitting in solitary confinement, he continued preparing for his eventual rise to power by reading volumes on politics, history, and economics. Years later he referred to this incarceration as his time spent at the "University of Ham."

Shrewdly judging that any bid for power would fail without the support of the masses, Napoléon recast himself in the image of a socialist and even wrote a book entitled *The Extinction of Pauperism*, seeing to it that copies fell into the hands of influential people around the country. A note he wrote, found years later in a copy of the book, read "Read this and tell me if you think it is calculated well enough to achieve my aims." During his years in prison Louis-Napoléon held one idea uppermost in his mind: the remaking of Paris. In early correspondence he wrote admiringly of Augustus, who had recast Rome from a city of brick into a city of marble. He envisioned that Paris, too, would become a symbol of imperial power that would dazzle the world.

After six years of confinement at Ham, Louis-Napoléon engineered an escape worthy of the Keystone Cops. During a period when repairs were being carried out in the prison, he disguised himself as a laborer, and with a wooden plank hoisted onto his shoulder to hide his face from the guard on duty, he walked out the front door to freedom. Safe in England, he watched events in Paris closely. When King Louis-Philippe was deposed in the revolution of 1848, Louis-Napoléon returned to Paris, and, riding on the mystique of the Napoléonic legend, was elected to the National Assembly. Less than three months later he was elected President of the Republic.

In December 1851, as the end of his presidential term approached, and with no chance of re-election because of a constitutional prohibition, Louis-Napoléon hijacked the Republic and declared himself President for a period of ten years. He abolished the constitution and dissolved the Senate, thus eliminating any power of the State to stop him. Ministers were rousted in the middle of the night and thrown into jail. Thousands of suspected opponents were arrested and shipped off to the French colonies. Government troops ran amok on the Grands Boulevards and slaughtered innocent men, women, and children with cannon, saber, and grapeshot. Victor Hugo provides a stirring account of this tragedy in his book *The Destroyer of the Second Republic Being Napoléon the Little*.

Exactly one year later, on December 2, 1852, Louis-Napoléon carried out the ultimate coup and declared himself Napoléon III, Emperor of France. The Empire was back. His reign lasted almost eighteen years. His fall from power was quick and ignominious in

▼ Napoléon III, the man behind the remaking of Paris. (photo, Riffaut, Mayer Frères, Niepce de Saint-Victor; Musée Carnavalet, ©PMVP/Negative offre)

the extreme. In 1870, the overly confident Emperor rode off with an army of 100,000 troops to do battle with the Prussians (remember the Franco-Prussian war?), determined to beat France's old adversary into submission. When a commanding officer was asked if his troops were well-equipped, he exclaimed, "Five times over!" Paris crowds, revved up with martial spirit, cheered the departing troops at the train station, shouting "To Berlin!" The air reeked of enthusiasm. At the battlefront, French hubris met the cold shower of reality and a humiliated Napoléon discovered how unprepared his forces really were: They didn't even have accurate maps of the war zone. On September 2, 1870, he surrendered at Sedan. Disgraced, he fled into exile in London. He never saw Paris again and died a broken man in 1873.

BARON GEORGES-EUGENE HAUSSMANN

When Napoléon III set out to fulfill his long-held dream of rebuilding Paris, he needed the right man to carry out his grandiose plans. The position within the city administration responsible for these matters was the Prefect of the Seine, then held by Jean-Jacques Berger, a man Napoléon knew to be lacking in vision, so he instructed his Minister of the Interior, the Duke of Persigny, to begin a search for a new Prefect. The business of interviewing candidates ended when Persigny met Georges-Eugène Haussmann. Here was his man. Persigny recognized in Haussmann a man who knew not only the technical aspects of the job, but who also had a ferocious enough temperament to take on the endless in-fighting of Paris politics. He described Haussmann as "one of the most extraordinary types of our time. Large, powerful, vigorous, energetic. Where the most intelligent, clever, upright, and noble men would inevitably fail," he wrote, "this vigorous athlete, broad shouldered, full of audacity and cunning, capable of pitting expedient against expedient, setting trap for trap, would certainly succeed."

On June 30, 1853, Haussmann took on his appointment as Prefect of the Seine. Persigny rejoiced at the prospect of throwing

this "tall, tigerish animal among the pack of foxes and wolves." At their first meeting Napoléon pulled out a large map of Paris criss-crossed with lines drawn in four colors. These were the new streets he wanted created. The different colors indicated the level of urgency for the various projects. Haussmann gazed upon the city that he would remodel like fresh clay in his hands. At the outset Napoléon wanted Haussmann to work with a commission of city planners, but after only one meeting the new Prefect managed to dissuade Napoléon of such an idea. From then on he worked single-handedly, answering only to the Emperor.

Haussmann remained in power for seventeen years. During that time he became one of the great power brokers of Paris, a position he reveled in and which earned him monikers such as Vice Emperor and Haussmann the First. When Napoléon fed his Prefect's unbridled ambition by making

◄ Baron Georges-Eugène Haussmann, Prefect of the Seine. Portrait attributed to Henri Lehmann. (Musée Carnavalet, ©PMVP/Negative Andréani)

him a senator, Haussmann took this cue to indulge himself further and added the title of Baron to his name even though he had only the slimmest of justifications for doing so.

The unprecedented scale of his building projects and the astronomical amounts of money required to carry them out led Haussmann to become a master at devising inventive and complicated strategies for raising money. To his credit, no new taxes were levied. Prime in his arsenal of financing techniques, along with the sale of municipal bonds and expropriated property, was the unorthodox practice of long-term loans borrowed against future revenues. Inexplicable financing, plus mounting debt and huge cost overruns, created a storm of controversy. To make matters worse, Haussmann hid much of his financial maneuvering, bringing greater suspicion and scrutiny.

In time, heaps of scorn rained down upon him. Not only did he draw barbs from those who were genuinely unhappy with what he was doing to Paris, but he also became a convenient scapegoat for everything wrong with the Empire. In 1867–68, Jules Ferry wrote a scathing series of articles ridiculing the Prefect—"The Fantastic Accounts of Haussmann"—a play on the title of the popular stage production *Les Contes Fantastiques d'Hoffmann*. In the end, Haussmann became Napoléon's albatross. The only way for the Emperor to salvage

▲ Rue d'Arcole. Created by Prefect Rambuteau in 1834, entirely demolished by Haussmann barely thirty years later.

his own power was to get rid of his Prefect. In January 1870, he dismissed Haussmann. But the Prefect would not go quietly: In an unprecedented act of defiance, he refused to resign and thus forced the government to fire him.

PARIS BEFORE HAUSSMANN

When Haussmann came to Paris in 1853, he found a city much smaller than it is today. The Paris of the 1850s was surrounded by a wall known as the Octroi, or Farmers-General wall. Constructed in 1791, it was a customs barrier with fifty-five gates of entry used to collect taxes on all consumer goods brought into the city. Beyond this wall encircling Paris was yet another wall around the city, this a fortification erected between 1841 and 1844. The area between the two walls was a

no-man's land of rude countryside and small villages, many with no more than hovels to shelter the inhabitants. In 1860 Napoléon III annexed the communes lying in this area, thus extending Paris to its present size. This annexation rendered the Octroi wall useless and it was torn down. The outer fortification remained in place until the 1920s.

The Paris that Haussmann was about to perform major surgery on was a city bursting at the seams, trying to fit onto a map that was medieval in size and layout. Despite its history and charm, Paris was dark, dirty, foul-smelling, and overcrowded. Aside from a few wide thoroughfares, the city was a tangle of narrow, twisting streets that made travel difficult at best, nightmarish at worst.

Though these streets are appreciated today for their picturesque quality, many people in the mid-1800s found them oppressive. One observer commented, "How ugly Paris seems after an absence. One suffocates in these narrow and humid corridors . . . the atmosphere is so heavy, the darkness so deep and thousands of men and women live, move, press together in these liquid shadows, like reptiles in a marsh." Another critic wrote, "All these windows and doors are so many mouths begging to breathe." Hanging over the city was a "leaden atmosphere, heavy, blue-gray, composed of all the filthy exhalations of the great sewer . . . Paris is an immense workshop of putrefaction, where misery, plague, and illness work in concert, where air and sun hardly penetrate."

The advent of the railway in the 1840s brought a flood of provincials into the capital. Between 1800 and 1850 the population of Paris doubled to over a million. The vast majority of these new Parisians were forced to live in conditions more squalid than they could have imagined. Property owners profited from the glut by sub-dividing large apartments into smaller ones. Single floors with high ceilings were cut in half by adding an additional floor in between. Formerly spacious courtyards were enclosed and divided up to create workspace for the many small cottage industries that sprang up. Living and work quarters became hemmed in with little light or fresh air.

The city's antiquated sewer system posed its own set of problems. Of Paris' 250 miles of streets, only eighty-seven had underground sewers that funneled into three large collector sewers dating from the Middle Ages. One of these sewers regularly backed up in bad weather, flooding streets and nearby cellars. The majority of streets had open sewers that emptied into the Seine running down the middle. Solid waste was carted off once a day from building cesspools, but other household waste found its way into the open sewers, emitting a noxious stench, particularly intense on hot days. Filthy splashes from passing carriages were a common annoyance.

Paris' water supply was just as inadequate. Only one house in five had running water, and of these only a handful had water piped to apartments above the first floor. A common sight in pre-Haussmann Paris was the thousands of water carriers delivering water to the city's inhabitants. Those who could not afford to buy water trekked to the many city fountains to collect what water they needed for the day.

More troubling was the source of Paris' water, the Seine, polluted because of the sewer waste that emptied into it. The poor hygiene in Paris led to the two great cholera epidemics of 1832 and 1849 that killed a total of forty thousand people. As early as 1749, the philosopher Voltaire pleaded for

an overhaul of the city. In *The Embellishments of Paris*, he described a "dark, confined, frightful" city in need of open space, wider streets, and an improved water supply. He knew that an endeavor on the scale he envisioned would require an extraordinary individual. Foreshadowing Haussmann by over a hundred years, Voltaire wrote, "May God find some man zealous enough to undertake such projects, possessed of a soul firm enough to complete his undertakings, a mind enlightened enough to plan them, and may he have sufficient social stature to make them succeed." One could say that Voltaire's God heard his plea.

PARIS AFTER HAUSSMANN

For seventeen years, Parisians lived under thick clouds of dust and amidst endless mountains of rubble. The figures Haussmann left behind are impressive. His army of 60,000 workers included 1,500 architects, 1,400 masons, 1,400 master carpenters, 1,500 master locksmiths, 500 master plumbers, 400 master chimney makers, 1,300 master painters, and 300 master roofers. The budget for the entire rebuilding of Paris was double that for all of Belgium.

For this expenditure, Paris could now boast seventy-one miles of new streets with the average width of streets at least doubled. 100,000 trees were planted. Four hundred miles of new pavement were laid. Before Haussmann, Paris had only forty-seven acres of public green space. In 1870 there were 47,000 acres, due largely to his creation of the Bois de Boulogne at the western edge of Paris, and the Bois de Vincennes at the eastern edge, in addition to the parks—Monceau, Montsouris, and Buttes Chaumont—within the city. The modern visitor can experience a pre-Haussmann street by strolling down Rue de la Harpe on the Left Bank in the Latin Quarter, or Rue Saint-Denis running through the site of the old central markets on the Right Bank. Both of these narrow streets were major thoroughfares used by travelers going north–south through pre-Haussmann Paris.

Haussmann's achievements underground were nothing short of remarkable. Two hundred and sixty miles of new sewers literally gave the city a new lease on life. The sewer system he built was so innovative that it became a must-see not only for tourists but for visiting royalty as well, including the Russian Czar, Alexandre II; and the King of Portugal. Haussmann also revamped the city's water supply. With Eugène Belgrand as head of the Municipal Water Works, Haussmann constructed an intricate system of aqueducts through the countryside to bring fresh spring water to Paris. Surprisingly, many Parisians preferred Seine water to the spring water, complaining that the new water lacked the desired "bite."

Pre-Haussmann Parisians had only twenty-six gallons of water per person for daily use. By 1870 this had increased to fifty gallons a day. Great as this improvement was, it did not solve the city's water problems. The number of houses with running water had quadrupled, yet half the houses in Paris were still without this convenience. But the groundwork had been laid, and in time Haussmann's successors were able to carry out his original aims.

▲ Rue de Rennes illustrates a key to Haussmann's transformation of Paris: the long, perfectly straight thoroughfare. (©ND-Viollet)

REACTIONS TO THE HAUSSMANNIZING OF PARIS

Civic improvements on such a scale come at a price, and many thought the price was too great. Haussmann's defenders were correct in pointing out the intolerable condition of the city, but many felt that these problems could be addressed without demolishing almost a quarter of the city. As one contemporary noted, "It seems that we can respect the jewels while changing the string, and sweep up without destroying the pavement."

Many Parisians objected to a central element of Haussmann's aesthetic: the long, straight thoroughfare. Condemning this mania for the straight line, they deplored the "mournful monotony" of the rows of perfectly symmetrical buildings. They lamented the loss of the old architecture, "the old moss covered gabled houses with their jutting eaves weathered by rain and smoke, hidden away among the old churches." The new buildings were "cold, colorless houses, as sad as prisons, and built as regular as an army barracks . . . all aligned like foot soldiers, strategically laid out, and because of this, so sad in their regularity." The Goncourt brothers, in their widely read journal of 1860, wrote of feeling like "a stranger . . . before these boulevards with their implacable straight lines without twists and turns that . . . make one think of some American Babylon of the future."

Haussmann demolished not only decrepit buildings but also many solid, well-built houses no more than fifty years old that still had a long life. The Prefect

◄ Demolition teams assaulting Paris. (Edmond Morin)

was not an artist or an architect; he was an administrator. "Architecture is nothing more than administration," he said. The altar at which he worshipped was that of efficiency. His underground works were so successful because there were no subtle aesthetic issues to work out. Aboveground, where these issues were everywhere, he simply did not see them.

Many, however, loved the new Paris. Art critic Théophile Gautier wrote, "The city is aerated, cleaned, made healthy, and puts on the makeup of the civilized world." Writer George Sand loved strolling down the broad new boulevards. But some years later, when the novelty of the straight boulevard wore off, Parisians began looking back nostalgically to the Paris they had lost. In 1885, Charles Garnier, architect of the new opera house, stated, "We do not want boredom to be the dominant factor in our new healthy city; we want original views which are incompatible with the odious abuse of the straight line."

The most often cited criticism of Haussmann was that he sacrificed Paris for reasons of military strategy. During the 1830s and '40s Paris had been convulsed by terrible uprisings that left thousands dead after intense street fighting. Narrow, twisting streets gave natural hiding places to the rebels and were easy to barricade. Wide, straight thoroughfares would give the advantage to the government, making it easy to move troops through the city or to fire a straight shot of cannon.

Criticism was still being leveled on this account as late as the 1950s. His preoccupations with hygiene, wrote one critic, were only "a convenient smokescreen . . . a sentimental alibi." What Haussmann and Napoléon would not admit publicly was asserted by others. Deputy Picard, admiring the new Paris said, "Now the artillery can maneuver with ease on a much wider field . . . Cannon balls do not know how to take the first right turn." It is significant that Haussmann strategically located new army barracks at the intersection of many of his new thoroughfares.

Some have suggested that Napoléon's best strategy against uprisings was the public works projects themselves. The army of workers he employed was made up of the same working class he feared. As long as they were putting bread on the table, they were less likely to foment revolution. A constant critic of the new Paris was the artist Honoré Daumier. His many satirical drawings show the plight of the Paris poor and point out the simple truth that once Napoléon gained power he let fall his pretense of being a man of the people and instead made life far more miserable for the working poor than it had already been.

The unrelenting demolitions created a housing shortage that sent rents soaring. Many whose dwellings were not expropriated had to move because they could no longer afford to live in them. Thousands of displaced people migrated from the city center to the villages surrounding central Paris, where there was little to greet them. Napoléon's claim that he wanted to clear the slums in the center of Paris only led to new slums at the city's edge. The modern phenomenon of commuting was born as many of these same people made the daily trek back into Paris to help tear down the very buildings they had been living in.

The success of Haussmann's new Paris aside, the truth stands that the remaking of the capital was a massive process of gentrification. As the poor were moved out, the wealthy moved in to occupy apartments that were unaffordable to the previous inhabitants of the quarter. Property owners facing expropriation sought to inflate the value of their property in order to bilk the government for the indemnities they were to receive. Shopkeepers painted their premises, stocked their shelves with empty boxes, and enlisted friends to fill the shop on the day the inspector was to come for the evaluation. In a popular joke of the period, two men meet on the street after a long absence. One man notices the other is dressed in the latest fashion with an expensive top hat. "What happened to you?" he asks. His friend leans forward and whispers, "I was expropriated."

HAUSSMANN'S BET

While many resisted Haussmann's renovations, the new Paris was successful beyond all expectations. The new city, sparkling in its embourgeoisement, became the pleasure capital of Europe, a mecca for those seeking the finer things in life, such as art, fashion, and fine cuisine. Yet, even though the city Haussmann created has achieved mythic stature, the attitude of the Parisians towards him has remained ambivalent. When he died in 1891, the suggestion that he receive a state funeral was rejected. The Prefect of the Seine at the time did not even attend the services. A statue created in his memory remained in storage for years and was only placed in public in 1989. It has taken generations for attitudes to change.

In 1991, on the centenary of his death, an exhibition honoring Haussmann was held in Paris. Exhibition organizers hoped the event would raise him out of the "purgatory" to which he had been relegated all these years. The title of this exhibition was "Le Pari d'Haussmann". There is a play on words here. The French word *pari* means "bet" and is pronounced "pahree," the same as *Paris* in French. Thus a double meaning: "The Paris of Haussmann" and "Haussmann's Bet." More accurately, though, it was Haussmann and Napoléon's bet, for the one cannot be separated from the other in the rebuilding of Paris. But while Napoléon's motives of self-glorification were dubious, and Haussmann's choices were often unfortunate in the extreme, the city they gave to the world—and its continuing hold on the imagination—is ample proof of who won the wager.

PARIS CONTINUES TO TRANSFORM

In the years following Haussmann's dismissal, the feverish pace of urban renewal in Paris slowed down but did not stop. Many projects begun by him were not finished for several years. The boulevard on the Right Bank bearing his name was only completed in 1926. The Boulevard Raspail on the Left Bank, begun in 1866, was inaugurated in 1913.

Despite the public works projects carried out in Paris during the early 20th century—streets widened, a block of buildings cleared—the character of the city remained largely unchanged. Then came the 1960s and '70s. Suddenly urban renewal on a scale unseen since Haussmann's time began altering the very nature of Paris. A striking example is the fifty-six-story skyscraper Maine Montparnasse built on the site of the old Montparnasse train station. The central market, Les Halles, located on the same spot in the center of Paris for over eight hundred years, was torn down and moved to the suburbs. Desperate pleas to keep Baltard's pavilions, the giant 19th-century glass and steel structures that housed the market, were ignored. When an American financier offered to buy these architectural gems and transport them piece by piece to the United States, he was turned down. Too impractical, said the French. One of these pavilions now sits in Yokohama, Japan, another in the Paris suburbs of Nogent-sur-Marne.

In the late 1960s, a stretch of the quai along the Right Bank was turned into a freeway. The quai along the Left Bank narrowly missed the same fate in the 1970s. In the white-hot fever of redevelopment a demolition permit was issued on the train station across from the Louvre, only to be saved at the last minute to become the popular Musée d'Orsay.

President Georges Pompidou loved *le moderne* and opened the door to the most aggressive entrepreneurs. His declaration in 1971 that Paris "must adapt to the automobile and give up an old-fashioned aesthetic" foretold of a sinister future. Throughout the 1970s, '80s, and '90s a juggernaut of development swept through the outer districts of Paris, erasing whole neighborhoods from the map and replacing them with massive apartment blocks. Belleville and Menilmontant in

▲ Le Corbusier's vision of the city of the future, a vision he wanted to carry out in Paris. (©Harlingue-Viollet)

the east of Paris, and the 14th and 15th arrondissements in the southern districts, are now carpeted with long stretches of bureaucratic concrete that bring the sadness of the suburbs into the city. Titles of books spell out a dramatic situation: *The Death of Paris, The Assassination of Paris, The Destruction of Paris.*

But the worst was avoided. Years earlier, in 1925, the architect Le Corbusier had put forth his own plan to modernize Paris. Known as *Le Plan Voisin*, it called for tearing down a large portion of the Marais. He deemed thousands of buildings in this area of the city "meaningless" and "insignificant," worthy only of demolition. In their place would stand a giant grid of eighteen skyscrapers, "events" as he called them, glass and steel structures that would carry Paris into the future. Fortunately, more moderate forces prevailed.

As Paris confronts the ongoing and inevitable pressures of growth and change, the same questions must be asked again and again. What price progress? How much of the city's history must be given up? To what degree are Parisians willing to compromise their quality of life? These and other questions are the crucible in which Paris continues to shape itself.

WALKS THROUGH LOST PARIS

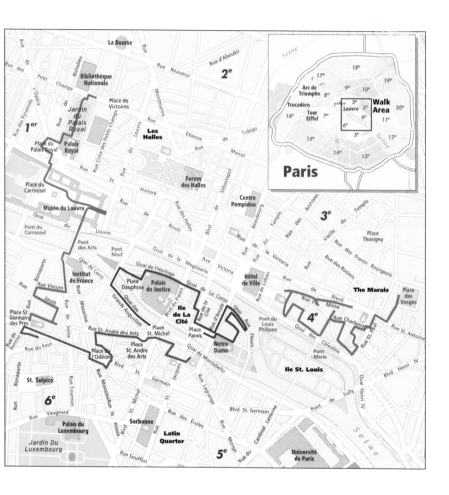

▼ Haussmann's Boulevard Saint-Germain and Rue de Rennes superimposed over old Paris.

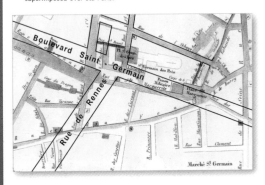

▲ Rue de l'Ecole de Médicine looking west from Rue Dupuytren. Everything here was demolished for Boulevard Saint-Germain. (photo, Marville)

▼ Map legend: Itinerary.

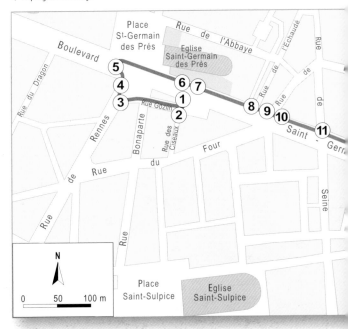

From Saint-Germain des Prés to Square Viviani

Starting point: Corner of Rue des Ciseaux and Rue Gozlin across the street
from the Church of Saint-Germain des Prés
Métro: Saint-Germain des Prés
Length of walk: Approximately 2 1/2 hours

The Boulevard Saint-Germain was one of Haussmann's proudest achievements and illustrates his concept of the modern city with its wide, straight thoroughfares cutting through the network of small, narrow streets of medieval Paris. To the careful observer, traces of the older city can be seen winding in and around the newer boulevards like, as Victor Hugo wrote, "lines of text in an ancient manuscript."

An east–west thoroughfare cutting across the Left Bank was a wish of Emperor Napoléon III, and to this end his first Prefect, Jean-Jacques Berger, began laying out Rue des Ecoles. When Haussmann came to power he insisted that a better location for this thoroughfare would be closer to the Seine. Thus he stopped all work on Berger's Rue des Ecoles and began work on Boulevard Saint-Germain. This newer boulevard was cut through in sections, with the eastern and western ends carried out first. The middle section from near the Church of Saint-Germain des Prés to Rue Hautefeuille near Boulevard Saint-Michel was only finished in the 1870s, after Haussmann had left power.

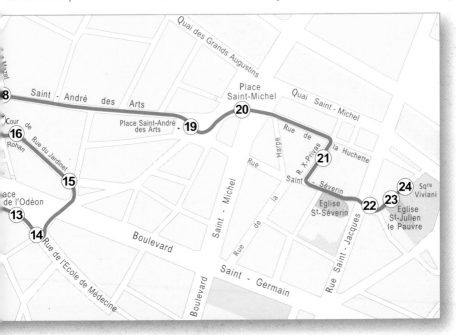

① Intersection of Rue Gozlin and Rue des Ciseaux

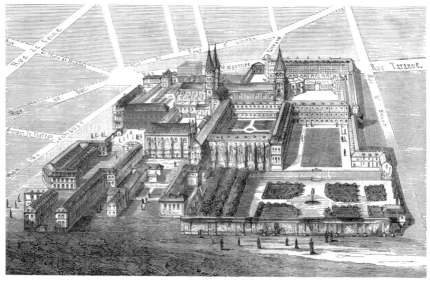

▲ Abbey of Saint-Germain des Prés. The south gate to the abbey, in orange, was at the corner of Rue des Ciseaux and Rue Gozlin, the starting point for this walk. In yellow, the abbey prison, demolished in 1854. See photo on p. 25. In green, the 16th-century Palais Abbatial in today's Rue de l'Abbaye, the only structure other than the church itself that remains from the old abbey.

▼ The abbey prison.

The Church of Saint-Germain des Prés is the oldest church in Paris and for many years stood at the center of a large abbey outside of a walled Paris. In the engraving, the church has three towers. Today there is only one. The two towers on the left were so damaged during the Revolution that they had to be dismantled. In 1368 King Charles V ordered the abbey to construct a fortification surrounded by a moat as a defense against the Normans. The south wall of that fortification ran along Rue Gozlin. The south entry into the abbey, colored orange in the engraving, stood at the intersection of today's Rue Gozlin and Rue des Ciseaux.

As hostilities abated over time, the wall was slowly dismantled. This engraving depicts the abbey in the 18th century when Paris had grown around the site and a fortification was no longer necessary. In 1637, the moat around the south wall of the abbey was filled in by order of the Parliament and Rue Gozlin was created. A year later, houses were built here. Numbers 1, 3, 5, and 7 Rue Gozlin are the original houses dating back to 1638.

Notice the yellow structure in the engraving to the left of the church towers. This is the abbey prison dating from the 17th century, demolished in 1854. It stood in front of today's 168 Boulevard Saint-Germain. Other than the church, the only structure remaining from the original abbey is the 16th-century

Palais Abbatial, colored green in the engraving, and standing in today's Rue de l'Abbaye.

During the Revolution, a terrible scene took place at the corner of Rue des Ciseaux and Rue Gozlin. On September 2, 1792, during the period known as The Terror, 168 prisoners of the Revolution—clerics, aristocrats, and common criminals—were herded out of the abbey prison by an angry mob and hacked and stabbed as they stumbled down Rue Gozlin to the intersection where you stand. From here they dragged themselves down the old Rue d'Erfurth and across the site of today's Boulevard Saint-Germain to the front of the church, where they were finished off and piled naked in a heap. In the carnival-like atmosphere of this macabre scene, the torn and bloodied clothes of the mutilated victims were auctioned off to the highest bidder.

Rue des Ciseaux dates from 1429. Houses at number 2, 3, 4, 5, and 6 date from the 16th century.

▲ View of the corner of Rue Gozlin and Rue des Ciseaux, 1868. In the foreground, Rue d'Erfurth. The first building on the right was demolished for the new boulevard. The two buildings on the corner date from 1638 and still stand. Compare the roofline of the building on the right above with the present building in the photo to the left below. Also, notice the lamp colored blue and compare to the photo on p. 16. (photo, Marville; Musée Carnavalet, ©PMVP/Cliché Degraces)

▶ Same view today.

▼ Antique dealer on the corner of Rue des Ciseaux and Rue Gozlin. Today a pizzeria.

② South door of the Church of Saint-Germain des Prés

Look across the boulevard.

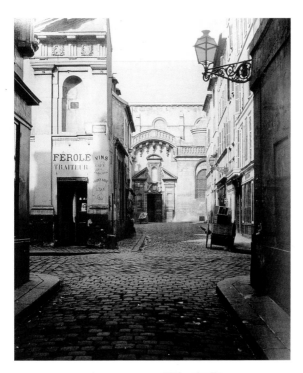

◀ View of the south door of the Church of Saint-Germain des Prés from the intersection of Rue des Ciseaux and Rue Gozlin, 1868. The blue lantern in the foreground can be seen on p. 15. The facade on the right with the orange lantern, in Rue d'Erfurth, is also visible on pp. 20 and 21. (photo, Marville)

▼ Same view from Rue des Ciseaux. Buildings in the foreground on the left and right are the same as in photo above.

Before the opening of this section of Boulevard Saint-Germain in 1877, the neighborhood around the church had all the allure of a village. Most streets in Paris were no wider. Moving through this labyrinth of narrow byways was extremely difficult, especially with the city growing so fast. While the modern observer is likely to find great appeal here, many Parisians of the period experienced only frustration. Relieving traffic congestion was therefore a central part of Haussmann's plan for the capital.

Rue de Rennes ③

Follow Rue Gozlin, cross Rue Bonaparte, and continue to Rue de Rennes.

The Rue de Rennes was begun in 1853 by then-Prefect Jean-Jacques Berger and was completed by Haussmann in 1866. The street was created in order to bring people from the Gare Montparnasse, then at the edge of the city, into the city center. In the late 1960s the train station, seen in the distance in this photo, was demolished and rebuilt several hundred yards back in order to accommodate the fifty-six-story skyscraper Maine Montparnasse, completed in 1972. This was Paris' first tall building in the city center. The lesson learned was to never do it again. The blight on the skyline was recognized as too great a price to pay for this much modernity. In March 1999, the mayor of the 2nd arrondissement in Paris called for the building's demolition. He said it was universally disliked, and had come to the end of its usefulness.

▲ Rue de Rennes in 1875. In the distance, the Gare Montparnasse. (photo, Marville)

▼ Same view today, dominated by the towering Maine Montparnasse skyscraper completed in 1972.

4 Cour du Dragon

Look across Rue de Rennes to the Monoprix.

▲ Interior of the Cour du Dragon, circa 1910.

◄ Monumental entry to the Cour du Dragon on Rue de l'Egout (Sewer Street). Designed by architect Pierre de Vigny, creator of the Hôtel Chenizot on the Ile de la Cité. On the left is Rue Gozlin. (photo, Marville)

Here before you stands a sad tale of urban vandalism, one of many examples in Paris. Until the late 1920s, this was one of the city's most picturesque corners. The Cour du Dragon was designed in 1732 by architect Pierre de Vigny, creator of the classic Hôtel Chenizot on Ile de la Cité. The passage became a mini–metal works housing small manufacturers of items such as wrought iron gates and balconies, and remained so into the 20th century. During the revolution of 1830, insurgents found a ready stock of metal objects here that they improvised into an array of weapons used during the uprising. Adorning the monumental entryway to the passage was a large winged dragon by the Polish sculptor Paul Ambroise Slodtz.

The courtyard survived Haussmann's restructuring of the quarter only to fall victim to the more modern taste of a later generation. The site was owned by a countess, a descendant of the original owners, who sold it in 1926. Plans for demolishing the Cour du Dragon caused a furor among conservationists, who argued for its preservation. Developers and architects of the new project promised that any new construction would incorporate the passage into its design. This was fine until the passage was demolished anyway. Only the large mutilated entryway was left standing. De Vigny's elegant creation stood for thirty years while discussion dragged on. Promises were made to incorporate the entryway into the new building. In 1943 the winged dragon was placed on the state list of architectural elements worthy of preservation. In 1957 it was dismantled and carted away to the Louvre where it can be seen today in the Cour Puget. The entryway was demolished shortly afterwards. By 1958 the new building, striking for its banality, was in place.

The more handsome facade you see today is due

▲ Cour du Dragon in demolition, 1926. (photo, Seeberger)

▲ The Monoprix before its renovation. A frightening view of what Paris might have looked like had Haussmann never carried out his public works projects.

▲ The Monoprix after its upscale remodel in 1999.

◄ Construction of Rue de Rennes. On the left, entry into the Cour du Dragon. On the right, Church of Saint-Germain des Prés.

▼ Vestige of the courtyard shortly before it was torn down in 1958. (photo, Pierre Jahan)

to a facelift completed in 1999. In the late 1990s this neighborhood went ultra-chic with boutiques the likes of Cartier, Christian Dior, and Pierre Cardin moving in, much to the alarm of local residents, who feared that the character of the quarter would be lost. In keeping with the more upscale character of the neighborhood, the floors above the Monoprix were renovated into luxury apartments, hence a new facade. Notice the reproduction of the winged dragon installed over the large arched doorway.

Strangely enough, the moribund Monoprix facade gives reason to rejoice. Had Haussmann never laid a finger on Paris, by the 1950s, the city would have been bursting at the seams and urban redesign would have been an urgent necessity. The city, in an effort to catch up, would have carried out massive demolition, and today's Paris would be lined with buildings in the style of the Monoprix instead of the more interesting Haussmann style of architecture. Despite his shortcomings, Haussmann's work can be seen as a pre-emptive strike, pulling the rug out from under the feet of the real barbarians.

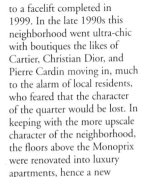

⑤ Saint-Germain des Prés

Cross Rue de Rennes and walk to the small traffic island on the Boulevard Saint-Germain. Look up the boulevard in the direction the traffic is flowing.

These two photos demonstrate the feverish pace of Haussmann's transformation of the capital. The Boulevard Saint-Germain is not yet complete, and a new building already stands on the right. Notice this same building standing before you. The row of buildings in the middle of the photo, also visible on pp. 16 and 21, is all that remains of the former Rue d'Erfurth. The buildings that stood opposite have been torn down in preparation for the new boulevard, which was completed after Haussmann left his post at City Hall in 1870. The church is visible on the left. Rue de Rennes, on the right, has been completed.

▲▲ Boulevard Saint-Germain, only partially completed, stops here at Rue d'Erfurth. (photo, Emonds)

▲ Same view today. Compare building on right with photo above.

Boulevard Saint-Germain ⑥

Cross the boulevard and walk to the south door of the Church of Saint-Germain des Prés.

Compare the photo above with the one on p. 16. This is the same street from the opposite direction; the colored lamps are the same. The spot under the blue lamp was the starting point for this walk. The buildings on the left are on Rue d'Erfurth, visible on p. 20, as well as p. 16. The awning on the right, colored blue, leads into Rue Childebert. Compare to p. 22. This street was designed with large matching fountains at its entrance. One of these fountains, seen in the photo to the far right, was saved from demolition and can be seen today in the Square Paul Langevin in the 5th arrondissement.

▲ Same view today.

▲ View from the south door of the Church of Saint-Germain des Prés looking towards Rue d'Erfurth and Rue des Ciseaux. The colored lamps are visible on p. 16. On the right is the entry into Rue Childebert. (photo, Marville, 1868)

▲ Fountain that stood at the entry of Rue Childebert, today in the Square Paul Langevin.

◄ South door of the church with the fountain at the entry into Rue Childebert.

⑦ Rue Childebert and Rue Sainte-Marthe

Look back in the direction of Place Saint-Germain des Prés.

◄ Rue Childebert in 1865. Blue overhang on left matches photo on preceding page. (photo, Marville; ©BHVP/Negative Leyris)

▼ Boulevard Saint-Germain, site of the old Rue Childebert.

Rue Childebert was created in 1715 by the Church of Saint-Germain des Prés as a means to increase the church's revenue. It was demolished for the construction of the Boulevard Saint-Germain. In a 19th-century account of this quarter, one of the buildings in this street was described as so dilapidated that dancing was forbidden inside. The Church of Saint-Germain des Prés is behind the buildings on the right. At the end of the street is Rue Sainte-Marthe (see next page), also torn down for the new boulevard.

▲ Rue Sainte-Marthe in 1865. Off to the right is Rue Childebert. The café Les Deux Magots is situated on this spot today. (photo, Marville; Musée Carnavalet, ©PMVP/Negative Degraces)

◄ Passage Saint-Benoît connecting Rue Sainte-Marthe with Rue Saint-Benoît, 1865. Note the sign on the right, SPECIALITE, visible in the photo above at the end of the street. (photo, Marville; Musée Carnavalet, ©PMVP/Negative Degraces)

⑧ Rue de l'Echaudé

Continue down Boulevard Saint-Germain to Rue de l'Echaudé.

◄ Rue de l'Echaudé in 1868. Match blue lamp to bottom photo on next page and to p. 27. (photo, Marville; Musée Carnavalet, ©PMVP/Negative Degraces)

Rue de l'Echaudé, like Rue Gozlin, was constructed in the 17th century on the location of the moat that ran around the wall of the Abbey of Saint-Germain des Prés. The main gate to the abbey was situated on this street at today's number 26. Many years later, this same address housed a brothel frequented by poet Guillaume Apollinaire and Alfred Jarry, author of the first absurdist play, *Ubu Roi*. The building on the left with the lamp colored blue was demolished to make way for Boulevard Saint-Germain. The building on the right, a fabric store in the 19th century, is a lively café today.

▼ Rue de l'Echaudé today. The building on the right is the same as in the photo above. Match the pattern of the windows in each.

► Boulevard Saint-Germain. The building on the left is typical Haussmann and was built as part of the new boulevard. The two buildings on the right are older and once stood on the old Place Gozlin, demolished by Haussmann. Match the building on the right with the red awning to the building on the right in the photos on the preceding page.

◄ Place Gozlin, today's Place Mabillon. The red dot on the map corresponds to the blue lamp on the preceding page.

▼ Place Gozlin, April 9, 1854. The abbey prison, seen here in the middle, is in demolition. On the right is the building with the blue lamp at the corner of Rue de l'Echaudé. (©BHVP/Negative Leyris)

⑨ Place Mabillon

Today's Place Mabillon stands on the site of the old Place Gozlin, one of the more unsavory spots in old Paris. From 1275 to 1636 this was the site of a pillory, an execution post where people condemned for everything from highway robbery to bearing false witness met a very public end. During the great religious wars, many Protestants died here.

▲ Place Gozlin looking east. The two men are standing on the balcony of a new Haussmann building at 168 Boulevard Saint-Germain. The building on the extreme right is also new. Notice the wide sidewalk, a novelty in 19th-century Paris. The building colored blue still stands and is visible in the middle of the photo below. At the bottom of the photo is the debris of the building with the blue lamp on pp. 24, 25, and 27. The street on the right is Rue du Four, in the middle, Rue Montfaucon, on the left, Rue de l'Ecole de Médicine. (coll. Paul Jammes; BHVP/Negative Leyris).

▶ Same view today. In the middle, Rue Montfaucon. The middle building on that street is the building in blue in photo above. The building to the left with each floor lined with balconies is typical Haussmann and is clearly different from the older building to the right.

Place Gozlin looking west towards the Church of Saint-Germain des Prés. Everything in this photo has been demolished except for the building on the extreme right with the sign wrapping around the corner of the building that reads ARIE AND OIS J; perhaps the first word is Marie. This is the same building seen on the right on p. 24, standing between Rue de Buci and Rue de l'Echaudé.

To the right, notice the building with the blue lamp. On the far left of the photo is a man facing the wall, perhaps the earliest photo of a man relieving himself in public. The horse and cart are standing on the site of the old abbey prison. The large sign on the wall, DENTS, advertises false teeth with a ten-year guarantee. If the reader could walk a short distance down the street in the middle of this photo, Rue Gozlin, he would find himself in front of the passage to the Cour du Dragon.

▲ Place Gozlin looking west towards the Church of Saint-Germain des Prés. Demolished for Boulevard Saint-Germain, 1868. (photo, Marville)

▼ Same view today. The corner of Rue de Buci and Boulevard Saint-Germain. This building is the same as the building on the extreme right in the photo above.

⑩ Rue de Buci and Rue du Four

Walk to the Rue de Buci.

1093. PARIS - Rue de Buci
vue du Boulevard St-Germain
C. M.

The turn-of-the-century photo of Rue de Buci above shows the overlapping of pre- and post-Haussmann Paris. Note the building on the left with the wraparound wooden sign. Match this to the building on the extreme right in the Marville photo on p. 27. The old fabric store here has become a café and billiard parlor.

The building on the right corner has been demolished, not to widen the street but to be replaced by a more modern building. While waiting for construction to begin, an ice cream stand has set up under the striped awning. Above the awning, the two posters advertising khaki hunting clothes are from the Belle Jardinière department store.

Note the woman on the left crossing the street wearing the large hat. What good posture.

▲ Rue de Buci from Boulevard Saint-Germain.

▼ Same view today.

Place Gozlin looking east.
On the left is the beginning
of Rue de l'Ecole de Médecine,
which led all the way to Rue
de la Harpe just beyond
Boulevard Saint-Michel. The
handsome building with the
people watching from the
arched window dates from
1724–26 and was designed
by architect Pierre Boscry. In
1854 Marville positioned his
camera in that window to take
his photo of the abbey prison
shown on p. 25. On the right
a butcher and his family stand
in the doorway of their shop.
Above them is a poster for
Madame Morin, first-class
midwife on this street since
1849. Off to the right behind
the butcher shop are Rue
Montfaucon and Rue du Four,
formerly Rue du Four-Saint-
Germain. Compare this to the
photo on p. 26 with the men
on the balcony. In that photo,
the butcher shop building
has already been demolished
in preparation for the new
Boulevard Saint-Germain.

◀ View of Place Gozlin looking east,
1865. (photo, Marville)

▶ Rue du Four-Saint-Germain seen from
Place Gozlin. On the right, the building
with the butcher shop has just been
torn down.

⑪ From Rue de Buci to Rue de Seine

Cross Boulevard Saint-Germain and look back across the boulevard.

This view of the old Rue de l'Ecole de Médicine was taken from the second-story window of the building with the blue lamp. See pp. 24 and 27. Notice the fabric store on the immediate left. The wraparound wooden sign is also visible on the corner of the building. Compare to pp. 27 and 28.

This portion of Boulevard Saint-Germain was completed after Haussmann left power. All the buildings on the right were torn down for the new boulevard. Haussmann had also intended to demolish the buildings on the left because they deviated ever so slightly from his cherished straight line. Notice that no two facades are on the same plane. This lack of uniformity rankled Haussmann no end. Fortunately, his successors were less rigid and left these buildings standing.

◀ Rue de l'Ecole de Médicine. The first street on the left is Rue de Buci. The second street in the distance is Rue de Seine. Compare the dormer colored yellow to photo below. (photo, Emonds)

▶ North side of Boulevard Saint-Germain between Rue de Buci and Rue de Seine.

◄ View of Rue de Seine, 1868. The cross street is Rue de l'Ecole de Médicine. The building on the extreme left and the first building on the right were demolished for Boulevard Saint-Germain. Match the building at the end of the street in both photos. (photo, Marville; Musée Carnavalet, ©PMVP/Negative Degraces)

▲ Same view today.

▼ Boulevard Saint-Germain showing Place Gozlin on left and the old Rue de l'Ecole de Médicine. In red, buildings Haussmann intended to demolish, but that were spared by his successors.

⑫ Odéon

Continue down the boulevard. Cross Rue de l'Ancienne Comédie and stop opposite the statue of Danton, a leader of the Revolution.

Cross the boulevard and go to the corner of Rue de l'Ecole de Médicine and Rue de l'Odéon and stand in front of the café Le Danton.

▲ The soldiers are walking down Boulevard Saint-Germain. Between the statue of Danton and the row of buildings is Rue de l'Ecole de Médicine. Notice there is not yet a cinema or an entrance to the Métro. Note also the café on the far right corner, still a café today, Le Danton. (postcard, 1906)

▶ Same view today. The inscription on the statue of Danton states that the statue stands on the spot where he lived. This is almost correct; his actual residence stood about one hundred feet to the left.

▲ View of Rue de l'Ecole de Médicine looking east. On the right with the red awning is the café Le Danton. Off to the left is Boulevard Saint-Germain.

◄ Rue de l'Ecole de Médicine looking east. This is Marville's photo of roughly the same view as the photo above. Everything on the left was demolished for Boulevard Saint-Germain. The buildings on the right still stand. Compare the pattern of balconies and windows in photos on this page. On the extreme left, notice the street sign for Rue de l'Ancienne Comédie. (photo, Emonds; Musée Carnavalet, ©PMVP)

⑬ Rue de l'Ecole de Médecine

Walk down to number 95.

▶ Rue de l'Ecole de Médecine. The arch colored blue is the entry into the passage Cour du Commerce Saint-André before it was cut in half by the new Boulevard Saint-Germain. At the end of the street, the house with the turret is where Jean-Paul Marat lived. (photo, Emonds; Musée Carnavalet, ©PMVP)

▲ The third arch on the south side of the street. Today a pizzeria.

This stretch of Rue de l'Ecole de Médecine is thick with the blood of the Revolution. Few people walking along here know the history they are trodding upon. Note the arches on both sides of the street in the vintage photo. The last arch on the left, colored blue, is the entrance to the passage Cour du Commerce Saint-André. Look across the boulevard and see this passage today, cut in half for the creation of the boulevard. The original entrance seen in the photo was only a few feet away, at approximately where the tree stands in front of you.

The most famous residents of the passage, living on the second floor, were Danton and his wife Gabrielle, hence the statue of Danton and the cinema bearing his name. In March 1794, Danton was arrested by the Revolutionary

Tribunal and guillotined five days later in Place de la Concorde. In his final message to his enemy Robespierre he wrote, "I lose my head at the moment that the Nation loses its mind. When it recovers, you shall lose yours." And he was right. A neighbor of Danton's in the passage was Camille Desmoulins, the fiery young lawyer who on July 12, 1789, delivered an impassioned speech in the Palais Royal garden making the first call to arms that led to the taking of the Bastille. He too lost his head on the guillotine, as did his pretty young wife, Lucille, a few days later.

Notice the house with the

turret at the end of the street. Jean-Paul Marat, firebrand of the Revolution, lived there. Anyone with even a cursory knowledge of the French Revolution knows that Marat was assassinated in his bath by Charlotte Corday. That event took place here. On July 12, 1793, Corday climbed to the second floor of this building and requested to see Marat, but his valet refused. Monsieur was ill, she was told. He was soaking in a tub to relieve his chronic pains. Corday returned the next day and again was refused entrance. From his bath, Marat heard the girl pleading and called out to let her in. Charlotte sat down on

▲ Entry into the Cour du Commerce Saint-André on Rue de l'Ecole de Médicine circa 1865. Notice woman vendor sitting in entryway. (©BHVP/Negative Leyris)

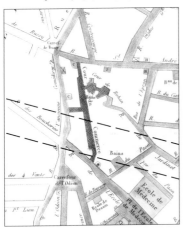

▲ Across the boulevard, the entrance into Cour du Commerce Saint-André. The original entryway into this passage was situated very near the tree in this photo.

◄ The passage Cour du Commerce Saint-André, with the outline of the Boulevard Saint-Germain superimposed in broken line linking Rue de l'Ecole de Médicine to Rue Saint-André des Arts before the construction of Boulevard Saint-Germain, circa 1865.

a stool next to the bath. "Mr. Marat, I have something that will touch your heart." Indeed. She pulled out a stiletto and stabbed him in the chest. The next day she was given a quick trial and lost her head on the guillotine. Jacques-Louis David portrayed Marat's murder in his famous painting, part of the Louvre's collection.

Marat published his incendiary newspaper *L'Ami du Peuple (Friend of the People)* from a printing press located in the Cour du Commerce Saint-André. Imagine him walking from his apartment to the arched entry leading into the passage. His house stood until 1876, when it was demolished in order to enlarge the school of medicine. What price progress?

⑭ Intersection of Rue Dupuytren

Walk to the corner of Rue de l'Ecole de Médicine and Rue Dupuytren.

◀ Jean-Paul Marat lived on the second floor of the building with the turret on the corner of Rue Larrey and Rue de l'Ecole de Médicine. Only the building colored blue, the medical school dating from the 18th century, stands today. Match this building with the same building in the above photo. (photo, Marville)

▲ Same view today.

▲ Marat's house in demolition. On the right, Rue Dupuytren. The houses on the right stood until 1903. (photo, Godefroy)

◀ View from a window in Marat's turret. The steeple of the Church of Saint-Germain des Prés is visible in the distance. On the right, a shop selling medical supplies. (photo, Emonds)

▲ Same view today. Notice church steeple in distance.

▶ The corner of Rue Dupuytren and Rue de l'Ecole de Médicine, 1901. This photo, taken some thirty-five years after Haussmann's work, gives an idea of what survived his urban rebuilding and what has been torn down since. These corner buildings were demolished in 1903 to enlarge Rue de l'Ecole de Médecine.

▲ Same view today.

◄ Rue Dupuytren towards Rue Monsieur le Prince. See this street in the photo above. (photo, Marville)

▲ Door at 4 Rue Monsieur le Prince, circa 1730–40. Visible at end of street in photo to left.

⑮ Rue de l'Eperon and Rue du Jardinet

Cross the boulevard and walk down Rue de l'Eperon to the corner of Rue du Jardinet.

▲ Rue de l'Eperon today.

▶ Rue de l'Eperon around 1870. On the left, Rue du Jardinet. On the right, Rue Serpente.

Rue de l'Eperon dates from the 13th century and was created as a link between Rue du Jardinet and Rue Saint-André des Arts. In its first three hundred years the street went through nine name changes. Its present name dates from about 1550. After comparing the two views, pre- and post-Haussmann, walk down Rue du Jardinet to the gate leading to the Cour du Rohan. Stop there and look back towards Rue de l'Eperon.

In the bottom photo by Marville on the facing page, a husband and wife sit comfortably with their child alongside their secondhand wares, waiting for customers. This is an unusual Marville composition since most of his images have no people— not because there weren't any, but because the film exposures were so long that they could not capture the people moving about.

◄ Rue du Jardinet from Rue de l'Eperon, 1865. At the end of the street is the Cour du Rohan. (photo, Marville)

▼ Same view today.

◄ Rue du Jardinet towards Rue de l'Eperon. The buildings on the left still stand. The right side has been entirely demolished. The last building on the left has a floor added on top. (photo, Marville; Musée Carnavalet, ©PMVP/ Negative Joffre)

▼ Same view of Rue du Jardinet today. Notice the typical Haussmann building at the end of the street on Rue de l'Eperon.

16 Cour du Rohan

Enter the courtyard at the end of Rue du Jardinet.

This charming spot consists of three small courtyards dating from the 14th century. Originally this was the residence for the Bishops of Rouen during their trips to Paris on ecclesiastical business. The composer Camille Saint-Saëns was born in the first courtyard in 1835. The building with the three small dormer windows on the top floor facing you in the second courtyard was built around 1550 by Henri II for his mistress Diane de Poitiers. In 1959 this charming spot came close to demolition. The owners of the courtyard, a large industrial enterprise, wanted to build something more modern and certainly more profitable. They were only stopped after vigorous neighborhood protest.

▲▲ Cour du Rohan circa 1900.

▲ Same view today.

◄ This elegant wrought iron tripod is a *pas de mule*, a step to aid in mounting a horse. It is the only one remaining in Paris.

⑰ Cour du Commerce Saint-André

Walk through the Cour du Rohan and exit into the passage Cour du Commerce Saint-André.

As you enter the passage, notice the first building on the immediate left, number 4. For many years this was a blacksmith's shop. A look through the window reveals a stunning relic of Paris history. Before leaving for the Crusades in the early 13th century, King Philippe-Auguste fortified Paris by building a defensive wall around the city that stood thirty feet high. Inside number 4 you can see a tower of that fortification, one of thirty-four that encircled Paris on the Left Bank. The blacksmith conveniently placed his forge inside this tower. The passage was created in 1735 on the site of the moat, which in 1582 was filled in. Originally the passage connected Rue Saint-André des Arts to Rue de l'Ancienne Comédie. In 1776 the passage was doubled in length and reached across today's Boulevard Saint-Germain to Rue de l'Ecole de Médicine.

Number 8 in the passage was the location of Marat's printing press, where he published his newspaper *L'Ami du Peuple* in 1793. In the basement of the corner building, number 9, Dr. Guillotin carried out experiments on sheep in his search for a machine that would execute people more humanely. He lived around the corner at 21 Rue de l'Ancienne Comédie.

Opposite the blacksmith shop is the back entrance into the oldest café in Paris, Café Procope, still in existence but only accessible from Rue de l'Ancienne Comédie. In 1670, the Italian Francesco Procopio

▲ Cour du Commerce Saint-André around 1920. The woman stands in the doorway of the blacksmith's shop. Note the sign of the key above. (photo, Pottier)

arrived in Paris and set up a stand to sell a new beverage, coffee. He opened his first café in Rue de Tournon in 1675 and moved to the present location in 1686. Five years later, the Comédie Française theater moved in across the street, assuring Procope success. In the 18th century his establishment became the favored meeting place for a host of luminaries including Diderot, Voltaire, Jean-Jacques Rousseau, and Beaumarchais.

A later generation of regulars included Alfred de Musset, Paul Verlaine, Balzac, and Léon Gambetta. Women of quality, not yet accustomed to entering such places, stopped their carriages in front and had their coffee brought out to them. Some years later, the Procope became a hotbed of political activity where many leading figures of the Revolution met. Another habitué during visits to the French capital was Benjamin Franklin.

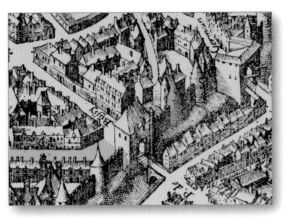

◄ Detail of the wall of King Philippe-Auguste. Merian map, 1615. Colored blue, the tower in the Cour du Commerce Saint-André. In yellow, Rue du Jardinet. In green, Rue Mazet.

▲ Interior view of the blacksmith's shop, 1958. The smithy stands with his back to the door leading into the oven he conveniently located inside the tower of Philippe-Auguste. (photo, P. Jahan)

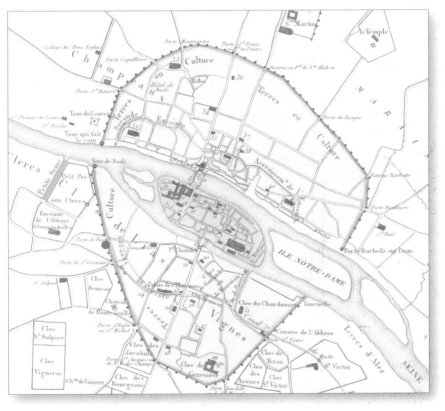

▲ Map of the late 12th-, early 13th-century Philippe-Auguste wall surrounding Paris. Red dot, the tower in the Cour du Commerce Saint-André. To the left of the wall outside of Paris is the Abbey of Saint-Germain des Prés. In blue, the canal known as the Little Seine, diverting water to fill the moat around the abbey. When this canal was filled in 1540 it became a footpath, and later Rue Bonaparte.

⑱ **Rue Mazet**

Exit the passage into Rue Saint-André des Arts and turn right. A few feet to your left is Rue Mazet.

This short nondescript street that holds little interest for the modern traveler was once a noisy, bustling scene with enough clang and clatter to raise the dead. For more than 250 years, an inn, the Auberge du Cheval Blanc, stood at number 5. The inn, a departing station for coaches carrying travelers to cities throughout France, opened in 1650 during the reign of Louis XIV and was demolished in 1907. In 1827 another coach station opened at number 3 with destinations in France, Italy, and Spain.

Adding to the life of this small street was a cabaret at number 7, Le Beuglant, which opened in 1852. Next door at number 9, the famed chef Magny had his restaurant, one of the most popular eateries in Paris during Napoléon III's reign. Many of the most notable writers of the period dined there regularly at Monday night soirées, including George Sand, Gustave Flaubert, and Théophile Gautier. Notice the large sign for Magny's restaurant on the side of the building on the right.

◀ Rue Mazet in 1865. On the right, halfway up the street is the Auberge du Cheval Blanc, demolished in 1907. (Musée Carnavalet, ©PMVP)

▶ Rue Mazet. For many years a university restaurant stood in the middle of the block. Today it is replaced by a dull building that, along with two other modern structures, only further diminishes the life of the street.

▲ The courtyard of the Auberge du
Cheval Blanc, circa 1900.

► Facade of the Auberge du Cheval
Blanc. A poster on the wall behind the
boy on the left advertises rides to the
top of a new attraction, the Eiffel Tower.

► Auberge du Cheval Blanc in
demolition, 1907.

⑲ Place Saint-André des Arts

Walk down Rue Saint-André des Arts to Place Saint-André des Arts.

In the 12th century, Rue Saint-André des Arts was a footpath bordered with flowers and high hedges cutting through a large vineyard known as the Clos de Laas. This pathway, a link between the Abbey of Saint-Germain des Prés and the city with its university quarter, became a street in 1179. In the 17th century, the building located at number 25 housed a cellar cabaret, to be frequented much later by Charles Baudelaire and his mistress, Jeanne Duval. The street is lined with many handsome buildings dating from the 17th and 18th centuries.

When King Philippe-Auguste built his wall encircling Paris around 1200, the abbey was suddenly outside the city, hence out of reach to many worshipers. To resolve

this problem, in about 1210 the king built a new church on the site of today's Place Saint-André des Arts. This church stood for almost six hundred years. In 1791, during the rabid anti-clericalism of the Revolution, it was closed and then demolished between 1800 and 1808. The site was turned into a *place* in 1809.

▲ Church of Saint-André des Arts.

▲▲ Place Saint-André des Arts in 1865. The large sign on the right advertises medical supplies such as mechanical chairs and beds for the sick and wounded. Signs on the left advertise public bath houses close by. These institutions were a part of Paris life into the 1970s. (photo, Marville; Musée Carnavalet, ©PMVP/Negative Habouzit)

▲ Place Saint-André des Arts in 1908, only a few hours before demolition of the buildings on the left for the new Rue Danton. (photo, Atget)

► Place Saint-André des Arts around World War I. Rue Danton is complete on the far left. A traffic island now exists to accommodate motor vehicles.

► Same view today. In an effort to restore livability to the quarter, the city is promoting urban design that favors pedestrians over automobiles. Thus the sidewalk has been recently widened, the street narrowed, parking has been eliminated, and the macadam removed and replaced with cobblestones.

㉟ Place Saint-Michel

Walk across the street to Saint-Michel fountain.

You are now solidly back in Haussmann territory. This fountain, designed by architect Gabriel Davioud, was completed in 1860 and provides an insight into Haussmann's aesthetic: Every thoroughfare needs closure, a visual punctuation point at the end of its perspective. Haussmann designed this fountain to provide closure to the perspective travelers viewed as they crossed the Boulevard du Palais on Ile de la Cité and approached the Left Bank.

Boulevard Saint-Michel obeys this same aesthetic principle. Completed in 1859, it was part of a long-held dream of Parisians for a north–south thoroughfare cutting through the city. Haussmann designed the boulevard with a slight deviation as it

▲ Saint-Michel fountain seen from Boulevard du Palais on Ile de la Cité.

▲▲ Place Saint-Michel around 1900.

approached the river so people traveling north would see the steeple of Sainte-Chapelle in the distance.

▲ A new Boulevard Saint-Michel
seen from Rue du Sommerard. Place
Saint-Michel, in the distance, is under
construction.

► Boulevard Saint-Michel towards the
Seine with the steeple of Sainte-Chapelle
closing the perspective.

㉑ From Rue de la Huchette to Rue Xavier-Privas

Cross Boulevard Saint-Michel and walk to the corner of Rue de la Huchette and Rue de la Harpe.

Follow Rue de la Huchette to Rue Xavier-Privas. Turn right and walk to the corner of Rue Saint-Séverin.

▲ Rue de la Huchette looking east from Rue de la Harpe.

▲ Rue Xavier-Privas today lined with buildings dating from the 18th century, all slated for demolition in Haussmann's grand plan for the quarter.

Look down Rue de la Huchette. Notice it begins wide and then narrows. The first two buildings were built by Haussmann. He had intended to demolish this quarter entirely and rebuild with new buildings and wider streets, but never achieved this goal. On many Paris streets the more modern buildings are set farther back from the street than older ones, with the expectation that when the older buildings are eventually torn down new ones will allow for a wider street.

In the 12th century Rue de la Huchette was the continuation of the footpath you walked along on Rue Saint-André des Arts. The footpath at this point became a street around 1210 known as Rue du Laas. The street took the name Rue de la Huchette in the year 1284. That's over seven hundred years ago!

Before Haussmann's work, Rue de la Harpe was one of two main thoroughfares running north–south through Paris. The other was Rue Saint-Jacques only a few blocks away. One comprehends the pressures Haussmann faced as he tried to bring the city out of the Middle Ages. The growing population created impossible congestion that made getting around Paris virtually impossible.

▲ Rue Zacharie in 1865, renamed
Xavier-Privas in 1929. (photo, Marville;
Musée Carnavalet, ©BHVP)

▶ Same view in 1910. A café-hotel has
claimed the space on the left.

㉒ Saint-Séverin

Go left at Rue Saint-Séverin to Rue Saint-Jacques. Cross the street.

▲ Rue Saint-Séverin at corner of Rue Xavier-Privas in 1868.
Note the taller building at the end of the street on the right,
a hotel next to the church. See this building in photo below.
(photo, Marville; Musée Carnavalet, ©BHVP)

▲ Same view today.

▲ Rue Saint-Jacques in 1908 before widening. The building
behind the tree is the hotel mentioned in the photo above. A
sign on the low building on the left announces big discounts
for reasons of expropriation. Street widening is imminent.
(photo, Atget; Musée Carnavalet, ©PMVP/Negative Ladet)

▲ Same view today.

▲ ▲ Rue du Petit Pont between the Seine and Rue Saint-Jacques in 1908. Recent demolition prepares the street for widening. Notice police headquarters building at the end of the street on Ile de la Cité, built by Haussmann in the 1860s. Compare to photo below. (photo, Atget; Musée Carnavalet, ©PMVP/Negative Ladet)

▲ Same view today.

◄ Rue du Petit Pont before demolition. Contrary to popular belief, the 17th-century building with the ornate balcony was not the residence of Madame de Pompadour. This street and its continuation, Rue Saint-Jacques, comprise one of the oldest thoroughfares in Paris, dating back to Roman times.

㉓ Rue Saint-Julien le Pauvre

Walk a few steps down Rue Galande to Rue Saint-Julien le Pauvre.

▲ Rue Saint-Julien le Pauvre. At the end of the street is the annex to Paris' main hospital on Ile de la Cité, Hôtel Dieu. Behind, notice the towers of Notre Dame.

▼ Same view after the hospital annex was demolished in 1908.

While the right side of Rue Saint-Julien le Pauvre has been demolished, the left side has remained untouched for centuries. Walk down to number 14. The sculpture on the arch provides a clue to the original resident of this house. Notice the reclining woman holding the scales of justice. At her feet is an olive branch of peace. The cherub holds an hourglass denoting the passage of time.

This house was the residence of Isaac Lafférmas, chief of police under Cardinal Richelieu in the 17th century. He was also Louis XIV's executioner. The cellars in this house date from the 14th century. In 1793, during the Revolution, when other prisons in Paris were full, this cellar was used to handle the overflow of prisoners.

Across the street is the Church of Saint-Julien le Pauvre, one of the two oldest churches in Paris; the other is Saint-Germain des Prés. Construction of this small church began in 1170 and was completed around 1240. This is one of about twenty churches that were built in the district around Notre Dame during the Middle Ages. Many of these churches were on Ile de la Cité and were demolished during or not long after the Revolution.

Through the centuries, Saint-Julien le Pauvre experienced years of great renown as well as years of total abandon. In 1524, infuriated students laid waste to the church after the unpopular election of a new rector. During

▲ The large building on Quai de Montebello is the annex to Hôtel Dieu. Behind it is Rue de la Bûcherie. (*Le Monde Illustré*, November 7, 1908)

▶ Same view of Rue Saint-Julien le Pauvre today.

▲ Detail of the entry into the house of Isaac Lafféémas at 14 Rue Saint-Julien le Pauvre.

the Revolution, the church became a salt warehouse. For years it served as a chapel for the hospital on Ile de la Cité, Hôtel Dieu. After being restored in 1889, it became home to Christian followers of the ancient Melchite rite of near eastern origin.

24 Square Viviani

Enter the garden.

Square Viviani, with its magnificent view of Notre Dame, was created in 1928 on the grounds of the former Hôtel Dieu annex. After these buildings were demolished in 1908, several ideas were floated about what to do with the empty site, including the construction of apartment buildings and a museum of Christian civilization. The latter idea went as far as having plans drawn up, but was derailed by World War II and never saw the light of day again. A view from the end of Rue Saint-Julien le Pauvre shows the striking difference between the garden today and the site circa 1910.

For a chaser to this walk, visit Shakespeare and Company, around the corner on Rue de la Bûcherie—a must for any American visiting

▲▲ Future site of Square Viviani, an unkempt yard while its future was still in deliberation. The tree, an Acacia, is the oldest tree in Paris, planted in 1601 by botanist Jean Robin.

▲ Same view today.

Paris, and the first place this author lived in 1963 after being thrown out of a distant uncle's apartment when he learned his nephew had come to Paris to study mime.

▲ Corner of Rue Saint-Julien le Pauvre (on right) and Rue de la Bûcherie (on left), site of the future Square Viviani. Notice that the building in the distance behind the larger building is also visible in the photo below.

▶ Square Viviani. The space between the two buildings across the garden is Rue de la Bûcherie. The portion of the street that extended to where this photo was taken was eliminated in order to extend the new square to the quai.

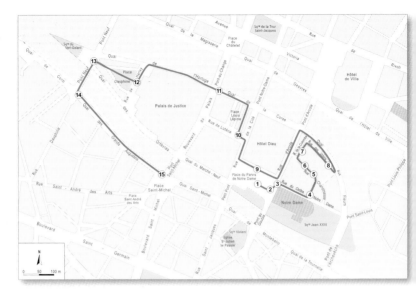

▲ Itinerary.

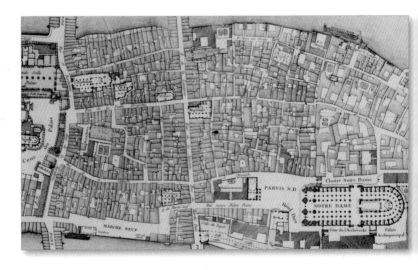

▲ This map shows the dense housing on the island before Haussmann nearly razed it completely. Not all the churches seen here were torn down by him. Saint-Denis de la Chartre (11th century), in red, was demolished in 1810; Saint-Landry (12th century), in yellow, in 1829; Saint-Pierre aux Boeufs, in green, in 1837. The Church of the Barnabites, in blue, was torn down by Haussmann to make room for the army barracks that later became the Préfecture de Police (Police Headquarters). The entries of the last two churches were salvaged and moved to other locations in Paris. The entry to Saint-Pierre aux Boeufs now stands on the Left Bank as the entry to the Church of Saint-Séverin. That of the Barnabites is now the entry to the Church of Notre Dame des Blancs Manteaux on the street of the same name in the Marais. (Delagrive map of Paris, 1754)

Ile de la Cité

Starting point:	Place du Parvis in front of Notre Dame
Métro:	Saint-Michel or Ile de la Cité
Length of walk:	Approximately 2 hours

If dirt could speak, the rush of voices coming from the earth you are standing on would tell enough stories to send you into a state of vertigo. For it was on this tiny island more than two thousand years ago that the city of Paris was born.

Physically, the island looked nothing like it does today. It was much smaller and, in fact, consisted of several small islands that over the centuries were joined together to make the present configuration. For an idea of how the island has grown, stand facing Notre Dame, placing yourself in line with the middle of the cathedral facade. Had you been standing near this spot in about the 3rd century, when this was a Roman city, you would have been teetering on the edge of the island. The island was also much lower; the Square du Vert Galant just beyond the Pont Neuf shows the island's original level.

At the far end of the square is a relatively new addition to Paris history, an archeological crypt. In 1969, workers excavating for an underground parking garage stumbled onto a hodgepodge of ancient foundations going back eighteen hundred years. Everything from 3rd-century Roman ruins to medieval houses and 18th-century buildings. Digging anywhere in central Paris is almost sure to reveal something of interest. Some years ago excavations for a parking lot on the Right Bank brought ruins to light dating back over a thousand years. Archeologists were given a pitifully short time to do their work before the bulldozers rolled in and laid waste to many valuable artifacts. In the case of the Ile de la Cité, the city chose wisely to conserve the site.

Haussmann's original conception of Ile de la Cité was to raze nearly everything except for Notre Dame and the Palais de Justice. His dismissal in 1870 thwarted those plans and left standing two-thirds of the houses on Place Dauphine, a few buildings next to the Palais de Justice, and a few houses on the north side of Notre Dame. It was perhaps this treatment of Ile de la Cité that earned him the moniker "Attila of expropriation," leveled by a contemporary. About fifteen thousand people were evicted from their lodgings on the island and banished to the outer reaches of Paris. These massive demolitions resulted in the construction of three edifices: the hospital (Hôtel Dieu), the Tribunal de Commerce, and an army barracks later to become Police Headquarters. Haussmann had intended to entirely demolish the Place Dauphine, but fortunately other priorities arose and he only tore down the houses on the east side of the *place.*

▲ Saint-Denis de la Chartre.

▲ Saint-Pierre aux Boeufs. The entry of this church was remounted on the facade of the Church of Saint-Séverin.

▲ Church of Saint-Séverin. Western facade.

① Notre Dame Square

Stand facing the cathedral.

◀ View from the top of Notre Dame, circa 1855. The island is still intact before Haussmann's work begins. In the distance, the Louvre, and on the horizon, the Arc de Triomphe. (photo, Bisson Frères, Bibliothèque Nationale)

▼ Same view in 1865. The houses in the foreground have been razed for the new army barracks, today's Préfecture de Police. The buildings on the corner of the Seine were spared by Haussmann but demolished in 1912 for the extension of the Palais de Justice. (photo, Achille Quinet)

Haussmann's demolitions increased the size of the square in front of Notre Dame fourfold, creating an ideal spot from which to view the cathedral. Yet this has remained one of the most criticized aspects of his work. Many believe that the cathedral, divorced from its surroundings, loses its scale and sits in the middle of what one critic called a "vast Siberian steppe." To this day the criticism continues. In a pamphlet published by the city and distributed in the underground crypt below the square, Haussman's design is described as extending the square "inordinately," leaving a cathedral that is "belittled." Haussmann would have disagreed, as a central element of his aesthetic was to isolate public monuments in order to better view them.

It's hard to believe, but Notre Dame was almost demolished after the Revolution. With anti-clericalism at a fever pitch, the cathedral was desacralized and converted into the Temple of Reason. Statues of apostles and saints were disfigured with hammers, gargoyles were destroyed, tombs were pillaged, and much of the cathedral's treasures were carried off. In this wretched state Notre Dame was auctioned off to the highest bidder with demolition its certain future. More sober minds intervened and halted this terrible fate.

Note the row of large standing figures spanning the facade. During the revolution it was incorrectly believed that these were the kings of France. The heads were subsequently smashed and cut off from the bodies. The heads seen today are replicas. In the late 1970s a water leak in the basement of a building near the Chaussée d'Antin revealed an unexpected treasure. As workers dug up the floor to get to the broken pipes, they found these lost heads, reportedly all standing and positioned facing Notre Dame. These originals now reside at the Cluny Museum.

For years the cathedral stood in a distressed condition serving as, among other things, a storehouse for large quantities of wine confiscated from the royalists. In 1803 it once again became a religious site, but with no restoration work undertaken, its condition continued to deteriorate. For Napoléon's coronation as Emperor in 1804, large tapestries were hung on the cathedral walls to hide the worst destruction. Then in 1831 Victor Hugo wrote *Notre Dame de Paris*. The success of this book rekindled a feeling of pride among Parisians for their cathedral, and in time plans for its restoration were put into motion. Restoration was carried out between 1845 and 1864 by Lassus and Viollet le Duc. The cathedral's spire dates from that period. The original was torn down in 1792 during one of the many attacks on the site. Notice the two towers of the cathedral and how they differ in width. The left one is slightly wider.

For a particular thrill, the traveler is invited to be on this square early on a Sunday morning when the cathedral bells are ringing. The sound itself is magnificent enough but becomes more meaningful if you can imagine that it is August 25, 1944, and Paris has just been liberated from five years of Nazi occupation. This is the same sound Parisians heard as they rejoiced at their regained freedom.

▲ View from top of Tour Saint-Jacques in 1867. The new Rue d'Arcole has been laid out and demolition is complete for the new main hospital.

▼ Notre Dame shortly after cleaning.

② Hôtel Dieu

Stand with your back to the cathedral and look across the square.

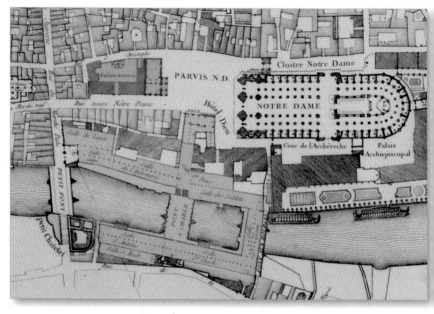

▲ In green, the foundling hospital. In red, Hôtel Dieu with the annex on the Left Bank. (detail of Delagrive map, 1754)

Hôtel Dieu was once situated on the water's edge between the Pont au Double and Petit Pont. This spot today is occupied by Charlemagne Square with its statue of the medieval king mounted on his steed, unnoticed by the great crowds.

Founded in the 7th century, the old hospital was demolished in 1878 following Haussmann's plans and rebuilt on the opposite side of the square. As of 2004, a fierce debate continues in Paris over Haussmann's Hôtel Dieu. The city wants to discontinue its use as a hospital and convert it to offices for the Palais de Justice. Much of the population protests.

Opposite the old hospital was the Hospice des Enfants Trouvés, a hospital for foundlings built in 1748 from a design by architect Boffrand. Large enough to have occupied about one-quarter of the present square, it was open day and night, receiving around eight thousand newborns a year. In 1838 the building was converted to the central administration offices for Paris hospitals. It was demolished in 1877.

▼ Hôtel Dieu in 1865 seen from Rue du Cloître-Notre Dame. On the extreme left is Notre Dame. The pillared structure is the chapel leading into the hospital that extends off to the right. In the distance is the annex to the hospital built on the south bank of the river, on Quai de Montebello. This is clearly visible in the map above. (photo, Marville; Musée Carnavalet, ©PMVP/Negative Degraces)

▲ Hospice des Enfants Trouvés. On the left is the old Hôtel Dieu. Marville took this photo standing between Notre Dame and the hospital. In the distance behind the hospice is the roof of the new Préfecture de Police constructed in 1865. (photo, Marville; Musée Carnavalet, ©PMVP/Negative Degraces)

▼ Same view today. In the distance, the statue of Charlemagne on the spot of the old hospital. On the left, the base of the north tower of Notre Dame. Compare to photo on opposite page.

▲ The square in front of Notre Dame framed by Hôtel Dieu on the right, and the Préfecture de Police across the square behind the crowds.

③ **Rue d'Arcole and Rue du Cloître-Notre Dame**

Look down Rue d'Arcole before walking down Rue du Cloître-Notre Dame.

The Rue d'Arcole was created in 1834 by Prefect Rambuteau as part of an effort to improve hygiene on the island in the wake of the cholera epidemic of 1832. Nineteen thousand Parisians died from the disease, and the mortality rate was particularly high on Ile de la Cité. Rambuteau's new street was laid out over two very old streets, Rue du Chevet Saint-Landry, and Rue Saint-Pierre aux Boeufs, visible on the Delagrive map on page 58. Little did Rambuteau know that his work would be obliterated. Haussmann often cited hygiene as the reason for his massive demolitions, but this was not the case here with buildings barely fifty years old. Today's Rue d'Arcole was completed in 1866.

▲ Rue d'Arcole in the 1860s. The left side, on the site of the future main hospital, is already in demolition. (photo, Marville)

▼ Rue d'Arcole today, redesigned by Haussmann.

The name Rue du Cloître-Notre Dame indicates the history of the neighborhood you are entering; *cloître* means cloister. At 18 Rue du Cloître-Notre Dame stood a large entry gate into the cloister of Notre Dame, a city within a city comprising all the houses between this street and Quai aux Fleurs on the north side of the island. For hundreds of years this was a sanctuary for the canons of the cathedral. Many high church dignitaries came from this cloister, including seven popes. The street was a dead end until 1804 when the last section was opened between Rue Chanoinesse and the quai to provide access to a bridge leading to Ile Saint-Louis.

The isolation of this small quarter ended with the Revolution when the gates were dismantled and the street was renamed Rue du Cloître de la Raison (Cloister of Reason). A number of buildings along the street survived Haussmann but were torn down around 1900 and replaced with more modern apartment buildings. The only house on the street pre-dating Haussmann today is number 16. In the 1960s, the tiny apartment with the barred window on the ground floor of that building was inhabited by a working class family as poor as church mice. As a student in Paris then,

I sold the *New York Times* to American tourists on this street as they descended from their tour buses. I also often lunched there with the family, whom I'd befriended. We lost contact and reconnected forty years later via the Internet.

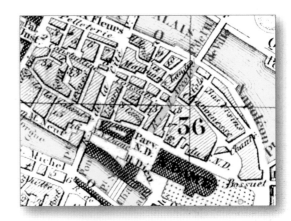

► Ile de la Cité, circa 1860. Rue d'Arcole, in red, was created by Rambuteau in 1834 on medieval streets Rue du Chevet Saint-Landry and Rue Saint-Pierre aux Boeufs. Barely fifty years later, Haussmann demolished the street to build something more in keeping with his urban plans.

◄ Rue du Cloître-Notre Dame seen from the cathedral square in 1865. All the buildings on the left were demolished. On the right, Notre Dame.

► Same view today.

▼ 16 Rue du Cloître-Notre Dame. The oldest house on the street, pre-dating Haussmann.

④ Rue Massillon

Turn left on Rue Massillon and walk to Rue Chanoinesse.

The scant remnants of medieval Paris on Ile de la Cité are in this tiny quarter you are entering. Haussmann wanted to erase all the streets and houses here but his sudden departure in 1870 put an end to these plans. Much of what he left standing was either demolished or greatly altered around 1908 when later urbanists set out to modernize the quarter. Number 8 Rue Massillon dates from 1740 and is the only old building left on this street.

▶ Rue Massillon in 1902. (photo, Atget; ©BHVP/Negative Leyris)

▶ Rue Massillon today. Second building from the corner, number 8, is the only old building on the street. Notice how the corner building has changed.

▶ Corner of Rue Massillon and Rue Chanoinesse. This house was a residence for the cathedral canons, and was torn down in 1959.

▲ Same view today with a modern apartment building in place.

▼◀◀ Rue Chanoinesse. Several rare vestiges of an older Paris that escaped Haussmann's demolitions.

⑤ Rue Chanoinesse

▲ Same view, circa 1900. Note the innovation of sidewalks replacing the *bornes*. The building in the distance at the very end of the street is a new Haussmann addition on Rue d'Arcole.

▼ Rue Chanoinesse today. The street was widened in 1908, eliminating many of the buildings on the left. The right side of the street is more intact. At the very end of the street is Hôtel Dieu, the hospital on Rue d'Arcole. The tall Haussmann building in front of it is partially visible in the photo above. The first building on the right with the flag is a garage for Paris' motorcycle police, built in the 1920s.

▲ Rue Chanoinesse, circa 1865. The two last buildings on the right are clearly recognizable today. The furthest one has a floor added on top. Notice the very short pillars at the base of the buildings. These pillars, called *bornes* in French, were common throughout 19th-century Paris and served to protect both pedestrians and building walls from wagon wheel axles. (photo, Marville; Musée Carnavalet, ©PMVP/ Negative Liferman)

◄ Rue Chanoinesse. Preparation has begun for demolition. Number 17, on the far left, will be spared. (photo, Godefroy)

▲ 17 Rue Chanoinesse today.

◄ Rue Chanoinesse in 1908. Demolition is complete for the street widening. Only the sidewalk remains to show the placement of the buildings and the narrowness of the old street. Numbers 22 and 24 Rue Chanoinesse are some of the oldest houses on the island and date from the 16th century. In earlier times they were residences for canons of Notre Dame.

▲ Same view today.

◄ 18 Rue Chanoinesse. This tower, the Tour Dagobert, dates from the 15th century and served as a light beacon for the Port Saint-Landry that stood a few feet away on the bank of the Seine. This five-story tower had a base no more than three meters square with a spiral staircase, made of a single piece of solid oak leading to the top, today on display in the Cluny Museum. The tower was demolished in 1908. Today the building houses a garage for Paris' motorcycle police. Notice the courtyard covered over with tin roofs, parasite structures typical of the period.

⑥ Streets Demolished for the Hospital, Hôtel Dieu

The construction of the new hospital, Hôtel Dieu, brought about the disappearance of a number of ancient streets on the island. One stands out for its remarkable history. Rue des Marmousets was the continuation of today's Rue Chanoinesse across the site of today's Hôtel Dieu. In the 14th century, two men—one a barber, the other a pastry chef, both located on this street—carried on a most bizarre business arrangement.

On given days the barber would let slip his razor and "accidentally" cut the throat of one of his customers. He would then transfer the body to the pastry chef next door via an underground passageway. Several days later, the pastry chef featured fresh pâté in his

▲ Rue des Marmousets, marked by red dot in map below, looking west at the corner of Rue Saint-Landry. (photo, Marville; Musée Carnavalet, ©PMVP/Negative Degraces)

▼ Delagrive map with dots representing streets that were leveled by Haussmann.

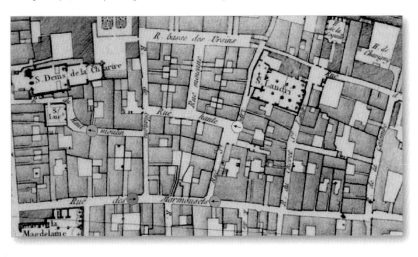

shop window. The scheme was uncovered when a dog, bereft of its owner, a German student, barked day and night in front of the barber shop. Suspicions were aroused and upon investigation by the police the two men were soon out of business. They were executed in front of City Hall and their buildings were razed to the ground. Nothing was built there for a hundred years.

▲ Green dot: Rue du Haut Moulin looking west. Note the panels attached to the front of the buildings. Also visible in the distance in the photo to the left. The purpose of these panels is still speculation. Were they to reflect sunlight? For security reasons? (Musée Carnavalet, ©PMVP/Negative Degraces)

▲ Blue dot: Rue des Marmousets looking east at the corner of Rue Perpignan. The street lamp on the right is the same lamp as in the photo on the opposite page. (photo, Marville; Musée Carnavalet, ©PMVP/Negative Degraces)

▶ Yellow dot: Rue Haute des Ursins. (Musée Carnavalet, ©PMVP/Negative Degraces)

⑦ **Rue de la Colombe**

Continue on Rue Chanoinesse to Rue de la Colombe and turn right.

One of the gates to the former cloister of Notre Dame stood on the corner of Rue Chanoinesse and Rue de la Colombe. The latter street has had the same name since 1223.

Note how Rue de la Colombe slopes down as it approaches the Seine and then rises up to meet Quai aux Fleurs. The quai was built in 1804 to protect the island from frequent flooding. Before it was in place, Rue de la Colombe descended straight down to the water. In fact, continue the slope of the street in your mind's eye and see it meet the water. This is the only place along the river in Paris where you can see the original shape of the land going back thousands of years. This is truly historic Paris.

Had Haussmann carried out his plans to demolish the houses between Notre Dame and the Seine he certainly

▲ Rue de la Colombe looking north. Note the band of cobblestones laid across the street. This marks the placement of a 4th-century Roman wall discovered during Haussmann's work along this street. The houses that stood on the left were demolished during the construction of Rue d'Arcole.

▶ Rue de la Colombe looking south from Rue des Ursins. (photo, Marville; Musée Carnavalet, ©PMVP/Negative Ladet)

▶▶ Same view today. On the left, Rue des Ursins. The corner building, 19 Rue des Ursins, contains remnants of the 12th-century Chapel of Saint-Aignan. The site was sold in 1791, during the Revolution, and houses were built upon it. It is a miracle that anything at all remains of the chapel. Of the twenty-three churches and chapels that once stood on Ile de la Cité, all that remain today are Notre Dame, Sainte-Chapelle, and these vestiges of Saint-Aignan.

would have leveled Rue de la Colombe. Leveling was an important part of Haussmann's redesign of Paris. The Tour Saint-Jacques on the Right Bank, for example, was once on a hillock. In a masterful bit of engineering this was leveled and the tower lowered. To create Avenue de l'Opéra, the Butte des Moulins, the hill from which Joan of Arc launched her attack on an English-occupied Paris, was leveled as well.

Coll. du Vieux Paris artistique & pittoresque

▶ Door to 4 Rue de la Colombe. Notice the difference in the decoration over the door in this photo and the one below right. The present-day doves in the latter are a modern creation replacing a bas-relief of a woman.

▼ 4 Rue de la Colombe.

▲ Detail of the entry to 4 Rue de la Colombe.

⑧ Rue des Ursins

Walk down Rue des Ursins. About halfway, turn around for a look at the street.
Then continue to the end of the street and up the stairs.

▼ Rue Basse des Ursins in 1860, today Rue des Ursins. (photo, Marville; Musée Carnavalet, ©PMVP/Negative Degraces)

▲ Rue des Ursins today.

◄ Rue des Ursins in 1900. (photo, Atget; Musée Carnavalet, ©PMVP/ Negative Ladet)

▼ Same view today. The building on the left was bought in the 1950s by oil baron the Aga Khan and redesigned à la middle ages in 1959–60 by architect Fernand Pouillon.

It is impossible to leave this spot without mentioning the house a few feet away at 9 Quai aux Fleurs. Built in 1849, it stands on the site of one of the great love stories of all time, that of Héloise and Abélard. In the early 1100s, Canon Fulbert lived on this spot with his niece Héloise, age seventeen. In 1118 the canon took in Abélard, age thirty-nine, to instruct young Héloise. The tutor was handsome and talented, a poet and musician educated in rhetoric and dialectic. Love between the student and teacher ensued. By the end of the year, Héloise delivered a baby. The canon, furious, had Abélard apprehended and—gulp!—castrated.

The two were separated; Héloise took up life in a convent, while Abélard went to a monastery. Their love endured for years through a correspondence that rings as fresh today as it did in the 12th century. When Abélard died at age sixty-three in 1142, Héloise had his body secretly transported and interred at her convent in Paraclet. She died in 1164, also at age sixty-three. The two lovers were placed in the same coffin and from there began a most circuitous voyage.

About three hundred years later, with the convent in ruins, their coffin was moved to a church in Petit Moustiers. In 1630, a well intentioned yet misguided hand separated their remains into different coffins and

▲ The future Paris home of the Aga Khan seen from Quai aux Fleurs. At the end of Rue des Chantres on the left, the steeple of Notre Dame. (©BHVP/ Negative Leyris, photo Atget)

re-interred them in a small chapel at a distance from each other. In 1701, a more compassionate mind brought their coffins together in this same chapel. In 1792 the bodies were placed in the same coffin but were separated by a lead partition and taken to a church in Nogent-sur-Seine outside of Paris.

In 1800, their coffin and monument were transported to Paris, to the Museum of French Monuments, where they were first buried in a garden and then moved to a courtyard. In 1817 the museum closed and they were moved for a short time to the Church of Saint-Germain des Prés and then finally to the Père-Lachaise cemetery, where they reside together to this day and hopefully forever after.

▲ Same view today. Notice the extent to which the house was transformed. The windows, for example, are completely different.

⑨ The New Hôtel Dieu

Walk along Quai aux Fleurs to Pont d'Arcole. Walk down Rue d'Arcole (look again at the photos on pp. 5 and 61) to the square in front of Notre Dame. Turn right and walk to the main entrance of the hospital, Hôtel Dieu. Enter and walk to the garden behind the information desk, then take the stairs to the top floor.

Haussmann's new hospital was begun in 1867 and completed in 1877. The Emperor's demand for a hospital of eight hundred beds was met with resistance by the Paris medical corps, which argued for a small infirmary of no more than 350 beds. A large hospital, they said, should be built on the outskirts of the city in a more pleasant setting. An eight-hundred-bed hospital on this small site would re-create the same stifling conditions, lacking in light and air, that Napoléon III and Haussmann were trying to alleviate in central Paris. Furthermore, there would be no room to lay out gardens for the refreshment of the patients who would be confined to a building across the street from something as doleful as an army barracks. But Napoléon understood the symbolic value of a large edifice in the center of the city and the message of wealth and power it conveyed. Work continued.

Midway through construction a commission of physicians inspected the hospital and reported that it fell short of current standards of hygiene and medicine and recommended that it be torn down. Building continued. Napoleon did relent, however, and agreed to reduce the number of beds to six hundred. Some years later, when both he and Haussmann

were gone from power, the top floor of the hospital was removed.

While the new hospital was under construction, the new opera house designed by Charles Garnier was also being built. Because work on the opera house had begun a few years before the hospital it was expected to be completed first. This posed a problem for Napoléon III. He did not want it to appear that a "monument dedicated to pleasure" had precedence over a "refuge for the suffering." He urged

▲▲ Site of the new main hospital, Hôtel Dieu, in the process of being cleared.

▲ Hôtel Dieu after the top floor was removed.

Haussmann to hurry work on the hospital and instructed the opera builders to do whatever it took to finish last. Nonetheless in 1875, two years before the hospital opened its doors, the opera gave its first performance.

▲ The courtyard of Hôtel Dieu, circa 1915. This space, a garden today, remained a parking lot until 1979. (photo, Henriseeberger)

▶▶ Same view today. A geometric garden fills the former parking lot.

▼ View from the work site of the new hospital, 1867. On the left, Notre Dame. On the extreme right, the foundling hospital. In the middle, the entrance into the chapel of the old hospital slated for demolition. In the distance, the dome of the Panthéon. (photo, Richebourg; ©BHVP/Negative Leyris)

◀ Same view today from the top floor terrace of Hôtel Dieu. Note the towers of Notre Dame on the left.

10 Rue de Lutèce

Exit the hospital and go right to Rue de la Cité.
Cross the street to Place Louis Lépine next to the flower market.

▲ Rue Constantine in 1858. In the distance is the Palais de Justice. A handbill on the wall on the left advertises a new invention, the pocket folding umbrella from America. (photo, Marville; Musée Carnavalet, ©PMVP/ Negative Degraces)

Rue Constantine was created in 1797 and began as a semi-circular plaza in front of the Palais de Justice. In its first stage this street extended only as far as the old Rue de la Juiverie, today's Rue de la Cité. Between 1838 and 1845 the street was extended all the way across the site of today's Hôtel Dieu to Rue d'Arcole. Notice the street's width and the condition of the buildings in the Marville photo above. This was modern Paris by any standard, with buildings in fine condition not much more than thirty years old when Haussmann tore them down.

In the Middle Ages the area from Place Louis Lépine to the Seine, and from Boulevard du Palais to Rue d'Arcole, was a Jewish ghetto. In 1180, King Philippe-Auguste expelled the Jews and confiscated their property. The expulsion erased all debts owed the Jews by the Gentile population, although the king demanded that all borrowers pay him one-fifth the sum they owed. Philippe-Auguste invited the Jews to return to Paris in 1198 after they helped finance his wars with England and Holland. Without property on the Ile de la Cité, many Jews resettled on the Right Bank along the Rue des Rosiers.

The Church of Saint-Barthélemy stood on Rue Saint-Barthélemy on the site of today's Tribunal de Commerce and was one of the few churches on the island to survive the Revolution. Shrines dedicated to this saint had been built on this spot since the 5th century. During the Revolution the church was made national property and sold off to become a theatre and later, in 1807, a dance hall, the Prado d'Hiver.

The Church of the Barnabites stood on the site of today's Préfecture de Police. Its facade was removed in 1863 and mounted on the facade of the Church of Notre Dame des Blancs Manteaux in Rue des Blancs Manteaux in the Marais.

▲ Rue Constantine in demolition, soon to be reborn as Rue de Lutèce. (stereoview)

▲ ▲ Rue Constantine looking east in 1860. On the right, the work site for the new army barracks. The top photo on p. 78 was taken from the end of this street. (photo, Marville; Musée Carnavalet, ©PMVP/Negative Degraces)

▲ Rue de Lutèce.

► The old flower market on the site of Place Louis Lépine. (S. Nash, 1829)

11 The Tribunal de Commerce

Walk through the flower market to Quai de la Corse and towards Pont au Change. Look across the river beyond Place du Châtelet and up Boulevard de Sébastopol to Gare de l'Est.

Paris. — Tribunal de Commerce

▲ Tribunal de Commerce, designed by architect A. N. Bailly and completed in 1860. In the left foreground, the tunnel for a portion of the new Métro is under construction.

▲ The oldest public clock in Paris on a tower of the Palais de Justice. (photo, M. Turin)

From this spot you can view the basic elements of Haussmann's aesthetic on a grand scale. The two keys to the urban design here are Gare de l'Est on the Right Bank and Haussmann's Tribunal de Commerce directly behind you. Were you a bird you would notice that the dome of the Tribunal de Commerce is off-center towards the Boulevard du Palais. The reason for this is that across the Seine Haussmann's predecessor, Jean-Jacques Berger, had begun laying out Boulevard de Strasbourg in order to bring travelers from the train station to the city center. But he only reached Boulevard Saint-Denis before being fired, and it was left to Haussmann to finish the job. Studying Berger's plans, Haussmann discovered a flaw. Haussmann's

aesthetic demanded that every long perspective have a focal point at its end to provide closure (see p. 48). Had Berger oriented his boulevard only a few degrees to the east, the thoroughfare, continuing to the river, would have had the dome of the Sorbonne in the distance to close the perspective. Haussmann, obliged to continue the Boulevard de Strasbourg as laid out by Berger, placed the dome of the Tribunal de Commerce off-center so that people traveling down the new boulevard towards the Seine would have it in view. The entire point is moot, however, as traffic on this thoroughfare is one-way, in the wrong direction. No one sees a thing.

For another example of Haussmann's aesthetic, look at a map of Paris and draw a line

► Flower market on Quai de la Corse.

▲ Boulevard de Sébastopol, created by Haussmann in 1855. In the distance, the dome of the Tribunal de Commerce.

between Place de la Bastille on the Right Bank and the Panthéon on the Left Bank. Haussmann laid out Boulevard Henri IV and the Pont Sully between these two points so travelers would see the dome of the Panthéon in the distance. But here too, traffic moves in the wrong direction and no one sees anything.

The clock tower on the Palais de Justice is the oldest public clock in Paris, first installed here in 1371, and rebuilt in 1574 and 1848. The bell in this tower played a crucial role in the infamous Saint Bartholomew's Day Massacre of 1572. Taking its cue from a bell on the Right Bank opposite the Louvre, this bell began sounding, thus signaling the beginning of the Protestant slaughter. Thousands were murdered in the streets, shops, on bridges, and in their houses. In 1793, Paris revolutionaries dismantled the bell and melted it down to erase this tragic memory. It was replaced in 1848.

⑫ Place Dauphine

Walk down Quai de l'Horloge and turn left at Rue de Harlay.

Place Dauphine, begun in 1607 and completed in 1616, was one of Henri IV's most important urban projects. Originally the Place had three sides and all the houses were built to a uniform design. Mutilations began as early as the 18th century as new windows were pierced and additional floors were added on top. Today the only houses faithful to the original design are the two houses facing Pont Neuf. As you face the Palais de Justice, notice the last house on the left. This is new construction completed in 1991. The east side of the Place was torn down in 1874, ironically to give a more impressive approach to the grandiose entrance to the Palais de Justice. A poor trade-off. The entrance has never been used and stands like an aborted American freeway of the 1950s, dead-ending in mid-air.

At least Place Dauphine still stands. Haussmann had planned to demolish it entirely in order to construct a new *place* in a Neo-Greek style. Like many of his projects, this one was thwarted by his departure.

▲▲ East side of Place Dauphine before Haussmann's demolition. (photo, Marville)

▲ Same view of Place Dauphine. Behind the trees, the Palais de Justice.

▲ The new facade of the Palais de Justice. Built between 1858 and 1865, this monumental entrance has never been used. (*L'Illustration*, November 4, 1876; ©BHVP/Negative Leyris)

► Houses of Place Dauphine facing Pont Neuf, before restoration in 1945.

► Same view today. The roof and dormers have been restored. The advertising signs have been removed.

⑬ Pont Neuf

Leave Place Dauphine and go to the statue of Henri IV on the Pont Neuf. Look over the bridge to Square du Vert Galant below to see the original level of the Ile de la Cité.

The western end of Ile de la Cité originally consisted of two small islands, Ile des Juifs and Ile aux Vaches. In March 1314, Jacques de Molay, leader of the Templars, was burned at the stake on Ile aux Vaches, the island nearest the Left Bank. In the 1570s these smaller islands were joined to the Ile de la Cité in order to allow for the construction of the Pont Neuf. This bridge had an ominous beginning. The first stone was laid by Henri III in a torrential downpour on Saturday, May 31, 1578. Accompanying him were his mother, Catherine de Médicis, and his queen, Louise de Vaudémont. The King was sobbing. He had just attended the funeral of his two favorite minions, who had died several days earlier in a duel. The king's sorrow led Parisians to name the bridge, for a time, Pont des Pleurs—the Bridge of Tears.

The Pont Neuf was completed in December 1605 under Henri IV and quickly became the center of public life in Paris. More than a bridge, the Pont Neuf was a promenade with an extraordinary street life made up of jugglers, mountebanks, ballad-singers, and entertainers of every sort, while an array of vendors barked, yelled, and hawked everything from fried fish to fruit, sausage, cakes, and assorted snake-oil remedies. Men ready to yank a tooth or clip your pet doggie for a few *sous* stood at the ready.

The bridge's success was due, in part, to the fact that it

▲ View from Place Dauphine looking west. On the right, the Louvre. (engraving, Aveline)

▼ Pont Saint-Michel, typical of Parisian bridges with houses from one end to the other.

was the first bridge in Paris to be built without houses on it. This was a real novelty for the time. In the 17th century, all bridges on the Seine were lined end to end with houses and shops that blocked any view of the river. People crossing a

bridge had no sense of leaving the land. On the Pont Neuf, Parisians saw their river as they had never seen it before.

The success of the new bridge brought about the invention of the sidewalk and curb in order to protect the crowds from passing carriages. In the 17th century, the round seats one sees today on the bridge were enclosed and contained tiny shops housing purveyors of the latest fashions. They were dismantled in 1849.

In the 18th century, the animation of the bridge spilled over to Place Dauphine, where public art exhibitions were held of Parisian artists who had been rejected by the Academy. These exhibitions became enormously popular. The government exerted strict control over these renegade exhibitions and granted the artists only three hours a day to show their work, from 9 AM to noon. Among the artists were Boucher, Chardin, and Fragonard, whose works now rate among the treasures of the Louvre.

▲ Pont Neuf, circa 1850. The half-circle seats on the bridge were once enclosed and occupied by sellers of luxury items. They were dismantled in 1849.

▼ Pont Neuf, circa 1900. The department stores La Belle Jardinière and La Samaritaine already stand on the Right Bank.

◄◄ Dog groomer on Pont Neuf.

◄ Pont Neuf seen from the Left Bank.

14 Quai des Grands Augustins

Walk over the Pont Neuf to Quai des Grands Augustins on the Left Bank and walk towards Pont Saint-Michel.

▲ ▲ Rue Dauphine in the continuation of Pont Neuf.

▲ Same view today.

The corner buildings at the entrance to Rue Dauphine were constructed in the 1930s by architect Joseph Marrast. Scientist Pierre Curie, husband of Marie, was killed by a delivery truck on this corner in 1906. His death was often cited as a reason for demolishing the older buildings to enlarge the intersection, improving safety. If this were so urgent, one wonders why it took so long to carry out the plan.

Rue Dauphine was created in 1607 by Henri IV in order to facilitate travel between the fashionable neighborhood of Faubourg Saint-Germain on the Right Bank and the Louvre. The creation of this street, along with the Pont Neuf and Place Dauphine, was part of his larger vision of embellishing this district. Henri IV's public works marked a departure from the closed medieval pattern to

the more modern concept of openness with public squares, unencumbered bridges, and wider, straighter streets.

Quai des Grands Augustins was the first quai constructed in Paris, in 1313, to allow King Philippe le Bel to travel from his palace on Ile de la Cité to his residence in the Hôtel de Nesle just beyond the Pont Neuf. As you walk along the quai towards Boulevard Saint-Michel, notice the restaurant Lapérouse across the street at number 51. This is one of the oldest restaurants in Paris, dating back to the 1780s.

For hundreds of years a large convent occupied the place along the quai where apartment buildings now stand. This most imposing structure, the Couvent des Grands Augustins, was built between 1368 and 1453 and extended from Rue de Nevers, just the other side of Rue Dauphine, to Rue des Grands Augustins. On the south, it reached Rue Christine. The convent had the largest assembly hall in Paris, plus a library with almost twenty-five thousand volumes. In 1789 the convent was made national property. It was demolished in 1797 and the land was divided and sold.

Anyone who enjoys walking along this quai owes a big *merci* to Valéry Giscard d'Estaing. Were it not for him, today's strollers would hear cars whizzing by on the embankment below. When the expressway on the Right

► Quai des Grands Augustins. This wide sidewalk would soon be cut back to favor automobiles.

Bank was opened in 1967, many were so pleased that they thought the same thing should be carried out on the Left Bank. Georges Pompidou was in power then and he loved *le moderne*. His famous statement that Parisians "must adapt to the automobile and give up an old-fashioned aesthetic" bode poorly for the future of Paris. Fortunately, upon Pompidou's death in 1974, the new President d'Estaing brought with him a more refined sensibility and quashed this project.

► View of Ile de la Cité in 1852. The island is still intact with the hospital, Hôtel Dieu, situated along the river bank. In the foreground, 17th-century Pont Saint-Michel, soon to be replaced. Beyond, note the bridge, Petit Pont, under reconstruction. In the distance, the passageway Saint-Charles over the river, linking the hospital to its annex on the Left Bank. (photo, Marville)

◄ Same view, circa 1900.

▼ Pont Saint-Michel in demolition, 1857. Built in 1616, it was lined with houses on both sides until the last one was removed in 1809.

20   PARIS. — La Place St-Michel et Notre-Dame — ND Phot

⑮ Pont Saint-Michel

At Pont Saint-Michel, cross the street and walk over to Saint-Michel fountain.

▲ View of Ile de la Cité from the Left Bank, circa 1860. The dome of the new Tribunal de Commerce is visible with space in front cleared and ready for the new Préfecture de Police.

▶ Pont Saint-Michel leading to Boulevard du Palais. On the left, buildings spared by Haussmann, but demolished in 1909 to enlarge the Palais de Justice.

▼ This wing of the Palais de Justice, with all the appearances of a medieval building, was built in 1912.

PARIS. — Le Pont Saint-Mich.

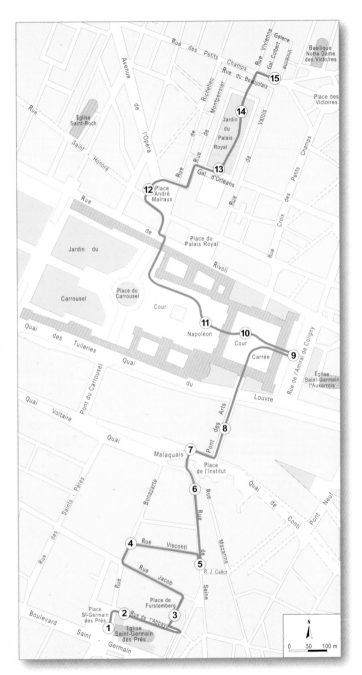

▲ Itinerary.

From Saint-Germain des Prés to the Palais Royal

Starting point: Place Saint-Germain des Prés
Métro: Saint-Germain des Prés
Length of walk: Approximately 3 hours

This walk begins in front of the Church of Saint-Germain des Prés, leads down to the Seine, over to the Right Bank, and ends just beyond the Palais Royal. Keep in mind that almost everything you see on the Left Bank portion of this walk was to have been demolished. The reason for this was Haussmann's plan for Rue de Rennes.

When Haussmann came to power in 1853, he found a Rue de Rennes, begun by his predecessor, Jean-Jacques Berger, that extended from the Montparnasse train station only as far as Rue de Vaugirard. Haussmann's plan was to continue it all the way down to the Seine. Fully expecting to complete the project, he expropriated all the houses standing in the path of the street's extension and designated, on paper at least, the lots of future buildings with their new street addresses. For this reason, the numbering on Rue de Rennes begins at Boulevard Saint-Germain with 41 and 48.

So certain did the Rue de Rennes extension appear to be that it is indicated on many early 20th-century guides to Paris. The project, in fact, was on the drawing boards until World War II. One of the more deplorable aspects of this plan is that it would have cut through and thus disfigured the Institut de France, a gem of 17th-century Paris architecture designed by Louis Le Vau, first architect to Louis XIV.

▲ The fortified Abbey of Saint-Germain des Prés. (Merian map, 1615)

① Place Saint-Germain des Prés

The Church of Saint-Germain des Prés was once the center of a large abbey that had grown up around a basilica established on this spot in the 6th century by Childebert I, the son of Clovis. In 1368, during the reign of Charles V, the abbey was enclosed by a wall surrounded by a moat fed with water diverted from the Seine and channeled through a canal along what is today's Rue Bonaparte. The walled abbey was bordered on the north by today's Rue Jacob, on the east by Rue de l'Echaudé, on the south by Rue Gozlin, and on the west by Rue Saint-Benoît. The fortification stood until the late 17th century, when the abbey was enclosed behind a simpler wall with large ports of entry.

Inside the church lie the remains of various personages, most notably among them

▲▲ Place Saint-Germain des Prés in 1865. Off to the right is Rue Childebert. The building colored blue still stands at the corner of Rue de l'Abbaye and Rue Bonaparte. The two buildings in front of it have been torn down. (photo, Marville; Musée Carnavalet, ©PMVP/Negative Degraces)

▲ Same view today.

the ashes of philosopher René Descartes. His head is located in the Musée de l'Homme, a fitting end for someone who spent his life preaching the separation of mind and body.

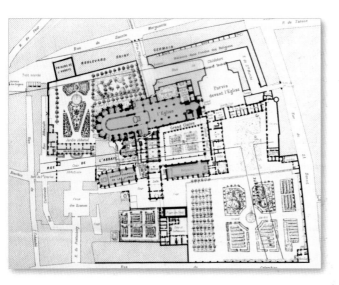

◄ This map shows the different periods in the abbey's evolution. The church is in blue. Its dependencies: in green, the refectory; in red, the Chapel of the Virgin; in yellow, the Palais Abbatial. Rue Childebert and Rue Sainte-Marthe have already been laid out, and the future Boulevard Saint-Germain des Prés, Rue de l'Abbaye, Rue Bonaparte, and Rue Saint-Benoît are superimposed.

▼ Square Laurent Prache. Remnants of the old abbey stand in this garden next to the church. Seen here, vestiges of the Chapel of the Virgin. This head of Dora Maar by Picasso, in homage to the poet Apollinaire, stood here for many years until it was stolen in March 1999. It was later found and returned.

② **Rue de l'Abbaye**

Walk down Rue de l'Abbaye to Rue de l'Echaudé.

▼ Rue de l'Abbaye in 1910. (photo, Atget; Musée Carnavalet, ©PMVP/ Negative Joffre)

▲ Same view today.

Rue de l'Abbaye was created in 1800 on land expropriated from the abbey. At numbers 6 and 8 Rue de l'Abbaye stood the Chapel of the Virgin, built around 1250 by Pierre de Montreuil, architect of Sainte-Chapelle on Ile de la Cité. At numbers 12 and 16 stood the abbey's refectory, built in 1239—a jewel of medieval architecture, thirty-seven meters long and ten meters wide with a vaulted ceiling fifteen meters high, plus fifteen stained glass windows. During the Revolution this site became a storehouse for large quantities of gunpowder, which exploded in 1794, destroying this five-hundred-and-fifty-year-old dining hall and badly damaging the Chapel of the Virgin next to it. Vestiges of the medieval dining hall were uncovered in the present-day buildings at 14 and 16 Rue de l'Abbaye.

During the period of the Terror in September 1792, this chapel was used to incarcerate the overflow of prisoners from the abbey prison, which stood on the site of today's 168 Boulevard Saint-Germain. On the night of September 2, all 264 prisoners, clergy and laypeople alike, were herded to the courtyard in front of the church and massacred. Fragments of the chapel were reconstructed and can be seen in the Cluny Museum.

The large building on the corner of Rue de l'Abbaye and Rue de la Petite Boucherie is the Palais Abbatial. This is the only structure other than the church itself that survives from the days of the abbey. The Palais Abbatial was built in 1586 by Cardinal Charles de Bourbon from a design by Guillaume Marchant. It was renovated in 1699 by Cardinal de Furstemburg. Among the abbots who lived here was Louis le Bourbon-Condé. Noteworthy was his affair with the ballet diva Marie Camargo, renowned for inventing the entrechat quatre, a complex ballet step.

The Palais Abbatial was expropriated by the state in 1790 and sold in 1797. It was then converted to a residence for artists, who set up their studios inside. Note the brick and stone construction. This was only the second building in Paris to use this type of construction. The first was the magnificent Hôtel Scipion Sardini on Rue Scipion. The 17th-century Place des Vosges was also constructed with this same combination of materials.

Rue de l'Echaudé was the eastern perimeter of the old abbey. The main entry gate to the abbey, with its drawbridge, stood at number 26. By the early 17th century this entry had been moved to the corner of today's Rue Gozlin and Rue des Ciseaux.

▲ The Palais Abbatial seen from the corner of Rue de la Petite Boucherie and Rue de l'Abbaye circa 1860's. (photo, Marville; Musée Carnavalet, ©PMVP/Negative Degraces)

▼ Same view today.

▲ A door to the Palais Abbatial. A handsome pastiche created around 1980 by the Office of Historical Monuments.

③ Place de Furstemberg and Rue Jacob

Backtrack to Rue de Furstemberg and the Place de Furstemberg, then to Rue Jacob.

Rue and Place de Furstemberg were laid out in 1699 by Cardinal de Furstemberg in order to give greater access to the Palais Abbatial from Rue Jacob. The stables for the palace originally stood on this site. Also in 1699, de Furstemberg created the adjacent streets, Rue de la Petite Boucherie and Rue Cardinale. Rue de Furstemberg took his name in 1815.

The most famous resident of Place de Furstemberg was the painter Eugène Delacroix. He left his studio on the Right Bank in 1857 and took up residence here at number 6 in order to be closer to the Church of Saint-Sulpice, where he had received a commission to paint several murals. Delacroix died here in 1863 at the age of sixty. In the late 1920s an entrepreneurial mind had the idea of tearing down this studio in order to build a parking garage. Delacroix supporters—artists and scholars—rescued the property and persevered until the state recognized the site's value and took it over in 1954. It was placed on the list of National Museums as recently as 1971.

The building facade next door to Delacroix's studio is the replica of an original facade that was torn down and rebuilt in 2000. This is a version of *facadisme,* where an entire building is gutted and the interior redone with larger, more modern apartments, and only the facade is left in place. Notice the bricks are imitation, painted on to resemble the original facade.

The northern wall of the Abbey of Saint-Germain des Prés ran along Rue Jacob. A person standing in this street in the mid-14th century would have had a clear view of Notre Dame, with nothing but open fields down to the Seine. Rue Jacob then was a footpath through those fields known as the Chemin du Pré aux Clercs. A short distance to

▲ ▲ Place de Furstemberg opening onto the Palais Abbatial.

▲ West side of Place de Furstemberg with its false brick facade and the addition of a third floor.

the east stood the beehive of the city enclosed by the wall of Philippe-Auguste, built about a hundred and fifty years earlier.

▲ ▲ Rue Jacob during the Great Flood of 1910.

▲ Rue Jacob today.

④ Rue Visconti

Follow Rue Jacob to Rue Bonaparte. Turn right and walk to Rue Visconti.

At first glance there is little here to entice the passerby. Yet this nondescript street is so charged with history, so thick with the dramatic lives of the towering figures who lived here, that whenever I turn this corner I'm surprised that I can walk here without having to muscle my way through the dense layers of emotion that have been laid down over the centuries.

Rue Visconti was created around 1540 from a footpath running through an open field and was originally known as Rue Marais Saint-Germain. The abbey wall was still standing then, so the first residents in this street lived practically in the shadow of the abbey.

Not long after the street was created it took on the name of Little Geneva because of the large number of Huguenots who took up residence here. A persecuted minority, the Huguenots practiced their religion in secret. But not secret enough. In 1569, a national synod held here was surprised by government soldiers. Four of the congregants were killed. One shudders at the thought of what took place here in 1572 during the Saint-Bartholomew's Day Massacre, when Catholics declared open season on Protestants and slaughtered thousands.

One of the most famous Protestants to live on this street in the 16th century was Bernard Palissy. Skilled in both the arts and sciences, he wrote articles on chemistry, mineralogy, and agriculture,

▲ Rue Visconti looking towards Rue de Seine.

and was the royal ceramist to Catherine de Medici. His assertion that fossils were the remains of living organisms was considered heresy.

Palissy escaped the 1572 massacre only to be thrown into the Bastille in 1589 at age seventy-eight. His refusal to convert to Catholicism brought the death penalty. Palissy was led to a burning pyre and given one last chance to renounce his heresy, to convert, and live. Slowly he undressed in expectation of death. His jailer, taken by the brave gesture of this old man, relented and sent Palissy back to his cell where he later died of starvation.

Over the door at number 24 Rue Visconti, note the sign that reads ICI MOURUT RACINE, 1699. (Here died Racine, 1699.) A small,

innocuous sign for a giant of French culture. One would expect trumpets blaring and flags waving to announce the home of this grand man of the theater. Oriented early on towards a life in the Church, Racine was born in La Ferté-Milon, fifty miles north of Paris. He discovered the here and now through his cousin, Jean de la Fontaine (the fables of La Fontaine), and the Abbot of Vasseur, a man of the church who was all too familiar with worldly pleasures. Straddling two worlds, Racine finally broke with the Church in 1660 and settled in Paris, where he began his career in earnest as a writer. His sonnets won attention at court and earned him the position of one of Louis XIV's favorites. By 1677 he was so sick at heart from the

► Rue Visconti in the 1940s when it was declared an insalubrious street by the Paris Health Department.

▼ Adrienne Lecouvreur, a brilliant tragedienne who only lived to the age of thirty-eight. (©BHVP/Negative Leyris)

▲ 21 Rue Visconti, October 1, 1885.

▲ Same view today.

backbiting and enmity of his peers that he abandoned the theatre all together. He severed all professional connections, married, and began fathering children, seven in all.

At 20 Rue Visconti, from 1836 to 1838, lived Prosper Mérimée, soldier, statesman, archeologist, and author. Few people know that it was his novel *Carmen*, written in 1845, that was adapted by Georges Bizet for his famous opera.

Next we meet the great Honoré de Balzac. At age twenty-six, this titan of the pen was as yet unsure of himself as a writer. He had published, but only under a pseudonym. Still searching, he thought he might become a publisher, and set up his own printing business on the ground floor of 17–19 Rue Visconti. He maintained a small apartment on the floor above. The money for this venture came from his mistress, Madame de Berny, twenty-two years his senior. Art and commerce often do poorly when sharing the same soul, and less than two years later Balzac was forced to abandon his print shop.

Eugène Delacroix lived in this same building from 1836 to 1844. The house at 16 Rue Visconti dates from 1682. In 1718 it became home to Adrienne Lecouvreur, grand diva of the French stage. Her elegant and natural acting style contrasted with the bombastic performances audiences were accustomed to and prepared her well for her Paris debut at age twenty-seven. Her immense

▲ Honoré de Balzac, who set up a printing business in Rue Visconti and failed. (©Photo RMN)

talent and presence on stage made her a cultural icon.

A few doors away, at 20 Rue Visconti, lived Lecouvreur's great stage rival, Marie-Anne Duclos de Chateauneuf. She moved to this house in 1729 at age fifty-five after a failed marriage to her seventeen-year-old lover.

Last is number 3 Rue Visconti. This building was constructed in 1749 and became a hotel in the 1820s, renting furnished rooms. In 1836, a Mr. Alibaud exited the hotel and walked to the Louvre. Strutting along with

his cane, there was nothing to set this man apart from other passersby. That is, until he reached his destination. As King Louis-Philippe exited the Louvre, Mr. Alibaud stepped forward and pulled out a pistol concealed in his cane and fired at the king. He lost his head for this misdeed, though the king survived.

Not a bad assemblage for such a small and unremarkable street. Before you leave, take one last look. With a little imagination you can see Racine in the distance returning home from

▲ Eugène Delacroix. (©Photo RMN)

a stroll with his children, or Delacroix walking to his studio, pensive, preoccupied with the canvas he will soon confront. Frédéric Chopin and George Sand walk to their portrait sitting with Delacroix. Balzac strolls by, worried as he contemplates his mounting debt. Mérimée strides down the street fresh from his recent trip to Spain and thinking of Carmen. How fitting it would be to acknowledge this street's mark on French culture by adding to its charm, perhaps by restoring the cobblestones.

◄ George Sand. (©Photo RMN)

⑤ From Rue Visconti to Rue Jacques Callot

At the end of Rue Visconti, turn right on Rue de Seine and walk to Rue Jacques Callot.

26 Rue de Seine was the site of a popular cabaret, le Petit Maure, established in 1618. The poet Saint-Amant died here in 1661. In recent years, the proprietor of the top-floor apartment of this building, a high-level city bureaucrat, added a floor above in violation of city building codes. The transgression was brought to the attention of a young lawyer fiercely dedicated to the preservation of historic Paris, Olivier Chaslot. With dogged perseverance he pursued the case, and in 1996 a decision by la Cour d'Appel de Paris obliged the owner to pay a fine plus undo the addition and rebuild the original roof with its dormers. The owner appealed the decision and not only lost, but had his fine doubled as well.

Rue Jacques Callot was created in 1912. Long before the street existed there stood a single large continuous block of houses. Then in 1823, a covered passageway was built here to provide a shortcut for pedestrians moving between the Pont Neuf and Rue de Seine and Rue Jacob. This was the origin of the Passage du Pont Neuf. The passageway was not a successful venture. Too far away from the more commercial streets and lacking any foot traffic, it languished in isolation. The only renown achieved by this site was in the pages of Emile Zola's first novel, *Thérèse Raquin,* where it was described in the most wretched terms. "It is paved with yellowish tiles that seem to excrete an acidic moisture . . . On beautiful summer days a washed out light falls into the passage from dirty windows and drags miserably through the corridor." Few regretted its demolition.

▲ ▲ Corner of Rue Visconti and Rue de Seine.

▲ Passage du Pont Neuf in 1910. (photo, Atget; Musée Carnavalet, ©PMVP/ Negative Briant)

▲ Passage du Pont Neuf in demolition for the new Rue Jacques Callot, 1912. (photo, Atget)

◄ Rue Jacques Callot today. Compare building at end of street to photo above.

⑥ Rue de Seine

Walk down towards the Seine.

In 1831, a remarkable personal transformation took place at 31 Rue de Seine in a twenty-seven-year-old woman named Aurore Dupin. Dupin, a confused mother of two fleeing a profoundly unhappy marriage, moved to this house and lived there for only four months. Uncertain of her future and determined to establish a more independent life for herself, she tried her hand at a number of things to earn a living: writing translations, painting snuff boxes, watercolor portraiture, and writing short stories for the Paris newspaper *Le Figaro*. By the time she left this address to live on the Quai Saint-Michel, she had begun wearing men's clothing and reinvented herself as writer George Sand.

For many years this same building was home to the Duncan Academy—run by Isadora Duncan's brother, Raymond—home of art exhibits, musical performances, and other activities. In the 1960s he could still be seen strolling these streets in his handmade toga, leather sandals, and long white ponytail, a hippy long before the term was invented.

The first houses on Rue de Seine were built around 1530. Previously this was a footpath leading to the river. The houses at 15 and 17 Rue de Seine date from the 17th century. The Rue des Beaux Arts was cut through in 1825. Oscar Wilde died on this street in 1900, in a hotel at number 13. Prosper Mérimée, mentioned earlier, and the

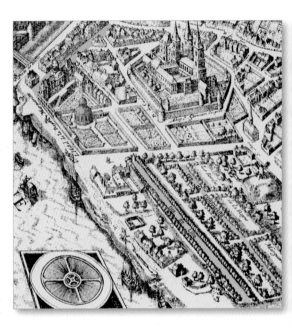

▲ The residence of Marguerite de Valois (Queen Margot). In red, Rue de Seine. The chapel, in blue, is part of today's Ecole des Beaux Arts on Rue Bonaparte. The garden footpaths, in green, became streets for future generations, Rues de Lille, de Verneuil, de l'Université, and de Beaune. (Merian map, 1615)

painter Corot lived at number 10 Rue de Seine from 1844 to 46. Fantin-Latour had his painting studio at number 8.

On this site stood the 17th-century estate of Marguerite de Valois, better known as La Reine (Queen) Margot, first wife of Henri IV. If the door at 6 Rue de Seine is open, take a look inside. The building facing you is a remaining portion of that once-lavish estate that extended over sixteen hectares.

The story behind the creation of Reine Margot's estate is most dramatic and illustrates how at times Paris urbanism has been driven by violent emotion (see p. 154 for more on the story).

In grief over the loss of her

Adonis, Reine Margot fled the Hôtel de Sens and moved to this spot on Rue de Seine where she built her own world free of unpleasant memories.

At her death in 1615, the queen left the property to Louis XIII who in turn sold it to pay off her debts. The section of the estate along Rue de Seine was parceled off and sold to developers. The houses that stand today at numbers 10, 8, and 6 date from that period. When the expansive gardens were

sold off in 1640, the garden footpaths became today's Rues de Lille, de Verneuil, de l'Université, and de Beaune. The buildings at 2 and 4 Rue de Seine were demolished in the early 20th century and the space became the small Square Honoré Champion.

▲ Facade of buildings between 2 and 10 Rue de Seine, behind which stood Queen Margot's residence. Access was through number 6. On the ground floor, the photo agency Roger Viollet is a Paris institution with a vast collection of several hundred thousand documents. (photo, M. Turin)

⑦ Quai Malaquais

Walk down Rue de Seine to Quai Malaquais and cross over to the river side of the quai.

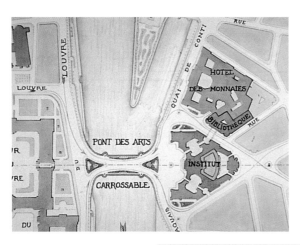

◄ Project for a steel bridge to be covered with ceramic tiles. 1903.

► Project for a bridge in the shape of an X between the Institut de France and the Louvre, designed by Eugène Hénard. 1904.

▼ Project for the extension of Rue de Rennes from the Church of Saint-Germain des Prés. (*L'Illustration*, May 1938; ©BHVP/Negative Leyris)

Here are frightening images of what you might be looking at had Haussmann's Rue de Rennes extension been carried out. The atrocious designs for the river crossing conjured up by urbanists obsessed with efficiency would have destroyed the Pont des Arts, one of the most pleasant pedestrian spots in Paris, creating in its place a speedway for automobiles. And to think this idea was on the boards until World War II.

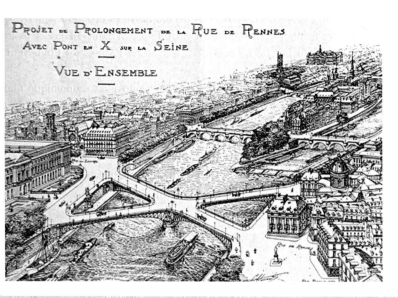

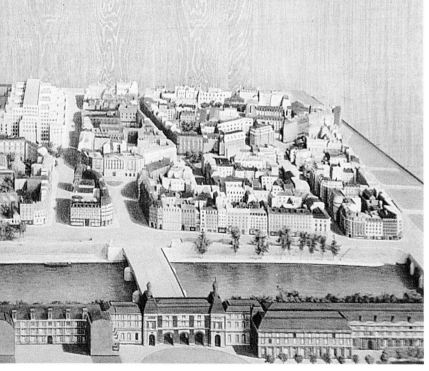

⑧ Pont des Arts

Walk to a point midway on the pedestrian Pont des Arts, and look back towards the Institut de France.

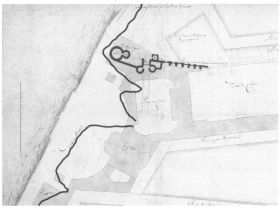

▲ View of the gate and tower of Nesle on the right. On the far left, Pont Neuf. In the middle, Hôtel de Nesle. (engraving, Israël Sylvestre; Musée Carnavalet, ©PMVP/Negative Ladet)

◄ Map of the Collège des Quatre Nations by Louis Le Vau. In blue, the tower and gate of Nesle at the end of the Philippe-Auguste wall. The red line is the old shoreline before the quai was built for Mazarin's College. (National Archives)

With a little imagination you can get an idea of what this view would have been like in the 17th century. Look closely at the engraving above. Notice the Pont Neuf on the left in the distance. In the middle of the engraving is the Hôtel de Nevers, built in the 1580s and demolished around 1641. Today, the Hôtel des Monnaies, the mint, stands there. On the right is the Tour du Nesle, the end point of the Philippe-Auguste wall where it

reached the Seine. This tower stood twenty-five meters high and was located on the site of today's Institut de France. On the far right is a bridge crossing the moat that surrounded the city wall.

The Institut de France was designed by Louis Le Vau and constructed between 1662 and 1674 from an endowment left by Cardinal Mazarin. Originally known as the Collège Mazarin and then the Collège des Quatre

Nations, its purpose was to house students of aristocratic families coming from the "four nations," or provinces, that had recently been annexed by France. In preparation for the construction of the college the shoreline along this section of the Seine was built up into a quai in 1662. This called for the demolition of the wall of Philippe-Auguste and the Tour du Nesle.

The placement of Mazarin's college here on the Seine seems like a perfect fit, with its majestic design open to the river. But things could have turned out differently. The committee appointed to consider locations for the college initially rejected this

site in favor of another near the Collège du Cardinal Lemoine. The directors of that college, however, refused to sell their land. The committee then moved to their second choice, the Jardin des Plantes, but this idea was rejected by Louis XIV. Le Vau once again pushed for this site on the Seine and the King approved, pleased at the prospect of having something so beautiful opposite his residence in the Louvre.

In Le Vau's original design, the two curved wings of the Institut housed twenty-seven shops occupied by skilled craftsmen, e.g., clockmakers, jewelers, and cabinetmakers. The shops were closed in 1804. In 1805, Napoleon transferred the Institut de France, then located in the Louvre, to this spot. The Institut is comprised of five academies, the most famous being the Académie Française.

Le Vau had planned for a footbridge across the river linking the college with the Louvre but that was only realized in 1803. The Pont des Arts was the first metallic bridge built on the Seine. Until 1848, pedestrians had to pay a toll of one *sou* when crossing. Opening day drew 650,000 people.

During a widening of the Quai de Conti between 1851 and 1853, the bridge was shortened by one arch. In 1979, the bridge was severely damaged

▲ ▲ Pont des Arts damaged in 1979 by a passing barge. It was entirely reconstructed minus one arch to give wider berth to barges.

▲ Pont des Arts and the Institut de France. To the right is the steeple of the Church of Saint-Germain des Prés. Further to the right is the fifty-six-story Maine Montparnasse.

when a barge struck one of its piers. The bridge was entirely torn down and reconstructed, although with one less arch, seven now, to allow a wider berth for passing barges.

⑨ Saint-Germain l'Auxerrois

Cross the bridge and pass under the huge arch of the Cour Carrée of the Louvre. Once inside the courtyard exit under the arch to your right onto Rue de l'Amiral de Coligny.

Looking across the street to the Church of Saint-Germain l'Auxerrois, one would have little idea that this was the spot where the infamous Saint Bartholomew's Day Massacre was launched.

In 1572 France was ruled by the weak and indecisive King Charles IX. Behind him stood his domineering mother, Catherine de Médicis. One of the king's closest advisors was the Protestant Admiral de Coligny. The Queen Mother, fearing that his influence was a threat to Catholic interests, manipulated her son into believing that Coligny had to be assassinated.

On August 22, Coligny was returning home from the Louvre when a failed attempt was made on his life. Wounded, he was carried home to the site of today's 144 Rue de Rivoli. Learning of Coligny's brush with death, Charles IX and Catherine de Médicis, feigning compassion, rushed to his bedside. "If the wound is yours, the pain is mine," said the king.

Protestants learned of the assassination attempt and rose up demanding revenge. The Queen Mother maneuvered her son into agreeing that the only way to prevent their own bloodshed was to spill the blood of others. On the night of August 24, 1572, Catherine de Médicis stood in a window in the Louvre and signaled to an accomplice across the way in the bell tower of the Church of Saint-Germain l'Auxerrois. At her signal the bells pealed

▲ Carnage of the Saint Bartholomew's Day Massacre.

and the bloodletting began. The sound of this bell was picked up by the bell in the clock tower of the Palais de Justice, thus assuring the continuation of the massacre on the Ile de la Cité and the Left Bank.

The first Protestant to be slain was Coligny himself. Raging mobs ran through the streets with sabers and pistols, murdering any Protestant in their path. Men, pregnant women, children, all were slain by the thousands where they stood. Pope Gregory XIII was pleased with the massacre and struck a medal to celebrate the slaughter.

Three hundred years later, when Haussmann was planning his demolitions for this area, it was suggested that he raze the church, but he would not hear of it. His decision came not out of any attachment to the building, but rather because he was Protestant; Parisians would see this as an act of revenge for the massacre.

Everything to the right of the large tower is the original church. To the left of the tower is the Mairie, or town hall, for the 1st arrondissement, built by Haussmann between 1857 and 1859. The tower itself, with a fine set of carillon bells, is often mistaken for the one whose bell signaled the massacre, but it is not. That signal came from three bells in another tower of the church, which is difficult to see from the street. Those bells were melted down in 1793.

Opera lovers are now in for a surprise. To the right of the church, Rue des Prêtres Saint-Germain l'Auxerrois was the birthplace of the opera *La Bohème*. In the 1840s, at number 17, stood the Café Momus, headquarters for many of the young Romantic poets. Among the regulars were Charles Baudelaire, Courbet, Victor Hugo, Honoré de Balzac, Nadar, Gérard de Nerval, and Henry Murger. Murger was a struggling young author

▼ The Church of Saint-Germain l'Auxerrois in 1852. The buildings on the left and right were demolished by Haussmann in 1854. (photo, Marville; Musée Carnavalet, ©PMVP/ Negative Habouzit)

◀ Same site after the tower and Mairie (town hall) had been built by Haussmann.

who wrote in the style of fantasy so suitable to the era of Romanticism. But a new realism was taking hold in literary circles. Looking to his surroundings for inspiration, Murger wrote a series of articles chronicling life in bohemia, drawing from the rich cast of characters in his circle. His girlfriend's name was Mimi. His friend Alexander Schanne became Schaunard. Jules Champfleury became Marcel. Murger himself became Rodolphe.

Scènes da la Vie de Bohème appeared first in a serialized version from 1845 to 1849. A literary portrayal of young artists living in abject poverty had enormous appeal to the very public whose values the bohemians rejected. Thirty years later, in 1896, Puccini seized on the continuing popularity of Murger's work and adapted *Scènes da la Vie de Bohème* for the stage.

Turn around towards the Louvre. The wing of the Louvre facing you, the Colonnade, was designed by architects Louis Le Vau, Charles Le Brun, and Claude Perrault. The moat surrounding this wing was a project of André Malraux, dug in 1964–66 when it was discovered to have been part of the original plans for the Louvre.

▲ ▲ Rue des Prêtres Saint-Germain l'Auxerrois. On the left, the church. On the right, the site of Café Momus. The building with the turret was demolished for the department store La Samaritaine. (Musée Carnavalet, ©PMVP/Negative Degraces)

▲ Same view today.

10 Cour Carrée of the Louvre

Turn around and walk back through the arch into the Cour Carrée of the Louvre.

There are few places in Paris with as long and continuous a history as the Louvre. Begun in 1202 and completed in 1993, the Louvre has been transformed from military fortress to royal residence, and finally to one of the world's great museums.

The origins of the Louvre are under your feet. The Philippe-Auguste wall erected around Paris, circa 1200, ran through the middle of this courtyard before ending at the Seine. To further protect Paris against the Normans, Philippe-Auguste built a fortress just outside the city wall. That was the Louvre in its earliest form. The fortress stood in the southwest quadrant of today's Cour Carrée and featured a crenellated wall punctuated with towers and surrounded by a moat. At the center of the square fortress stood a large tower thirty-two meters high, surrounded by a second moat. This tower was visible for miles around and was recognized throughout France as an imposing symbol of royal power. It had several levels inside and was used to house the Royal Treasury as well as to hold prisoners of high rank.

In 1984–85, excavations in the Cour Carrée revealed stunning remains of Philippe-Auguste's medieval fortress, including foundation walls for the moat and tower. They can be visited inside the Louvre and are well worth the visit.

By 1358, as Paris continued to expand, Charles V built a new wall around the city

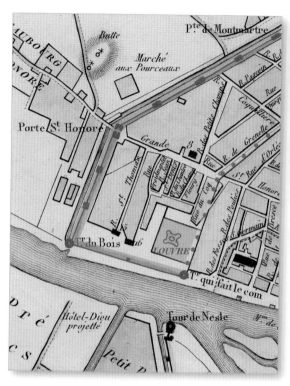

▲ The Louvre, in orange, stands next to the Philippe-Auguste wall after the construction of the Charles V wall in blue.

several hundred yards beyond the wall of Philippe-Auguste. He might have decided to tear down the fortress, now within the city and having no strategic value. How different Paris would have been today. Instead he decided to convert the fortress into a royal residence and undertook a massive renovation to give the medieval site a more magnificent air. Height was added to allow for spacious royal apartments. Turrets topped with flags, colorful

banners, and gold-colored weathervanes were built to give the roofline a more festive appearance. Decorative embellishments were added, including gargoyles and statues carved by France's finest sculptors. Gardens were laid out. Windows were cut into walls to bring more light.

But the monarchs to follow Charles V chose instead to live in their châteaux in the Loire. When they did visit the capital they preferred to stay at the Hôtel des Tournelles in

the Marais. Consequently, the Louvre fell from its status as palace to become little more than a prison and at times an arsenal. Rooms that once resonated with the chatter of royalty stood mute, housing only artillery and munitions.

The fortunes of the Louvre improved in 1527 when Francois I announced that he wanted to establish his court here. A man of arts and letters as well as a warrior, Francois I introduced the Renaissance to the French court. His exposure to the culture of Italy through the many wars he waged there made him a great admirer of Italian artists. Leonardo da Vinci came to France at his invitation and, in fact, died in his arms in Paris.

In a desire to modernize the Louvre, Francois I tore down the medieval tower in 1528 and filled in the moat. He also built up the shoreline along the river to form a quai, today's Quai du Louvre. In 1546, a year before his

▲ View of the foundations of Philippe-Auguste's 13th-century Louvre in the lower level of today's Louvre. (photo, J. LeBar)

▼ Philippe-Auguste's wall cuts through the large Cour Carrée, with the original Louvre in black. (Berty, *Topographie Historique du Vieux Paris*)

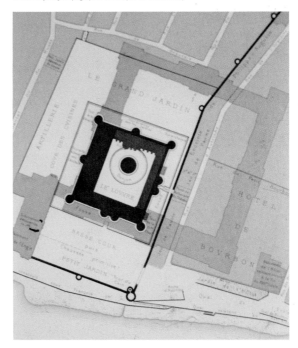

death, Francois I called upon architect Pierre Lescot to build a truly splendid palace. Lescot continued work on the Louvre through the reigns of Henri II, Charles IX, and into the reign of Henri III, tearing down sections of the medieval Louvre to rebuild in a more contemporary Renaissance style.

Lescot's work, in fact, is right in front of you. Face in the direction of the pyramid, towards the west wing of the Cour Carrée. Notice the large archway and the large dome above it. This is the Pavillon de l'Horloge, also known as the Pavillon Sully. Everything to the left of the dome, plus a portion of the south wing on the Seine side, is Lescot's design. The dome itself was built later. By the time of Lescot's death in 1578, the Louvre was still only a quarter the size of today's Cour Carrée

and stood as a hodgepodge of architectural styles, with the newer Renaissance facades staring at Gothic facades just across the courtyard.

It was Henri IV, Paris's first real urbanist, who, around 1600, conceived of enlarging this small medieval courtyard into today's larger Cour Carrée. But it took his son, Louis XIII, to begin the project. In 1624 he tore down the north wing of Charles V's Louvre, and with architect Jacques Lemercier built both the Pavillon de l'Horloge and the rest of the wing in the style of Lescot to create the continuous facade you see today. He also turned the corner and began the north wing, but only completed it halfway.

When Louis XIII died in 1643 he left a huge construction site. All work on the Louvre ceased when Anne of Austria and the

five-year-old dauphin, Louis XIV, moved to the Palais Royal, leaving the Louvre empty once again. Nine years later, the Queen Mother and her son, now fourteen years old, returned and took up residence in the Lescot wing.

In 1660, Louis XIV undertook to complete the Cour Carrée. With architect Louis Le Vau directing the project he tore down the last vestiges of the medieval Louvre and enclosed the Cour Carrée with wings matching Lescot's design. But the work was far from done. The facade on the side of Rue de l'Amiral Coligny was unfinished. Because this wing faced the city it was decided that it would serve as the main entrance, the *porte d'honneur*. The design of the facade and the entrance, therefore, were of immense importance and needed the requisite pomp suitable for royalty. Proposals were submitted by Le Vau, Lemercier, and François Mansart, and what ensued can only be called a fiasco.

Louis XIV's minister Colbert rejected all the proposals. Worse yet, and an insult to the French architects, Colbert invited the Italian architect Bernini to Paris in 1665 to undertake the project. Bernini was a man of no small ego. After a sumptuous welcome he summarily dismissed all previous work and advised tearing everything down, even the original Lescot wing. The work was to begin from scratch. Some diplomatic maneuvering from the French convinced Bernini to confine his ideas only to the east wing,

▲ The Louvre of Charles V represented in *Les très riches heures du duc de Berry.*
(©Photo RMN)

the facade facing the city. He agreed, but his designs were so inappropriate that no one took them seriously, yet no one had the audacity to tell him so. The French then resorted to the only reasonable course of action. A ceremony of pomp and circumstance was held on the site to mark the laying of the first stone of Bernini's facade. After many pronouncements, salutations, and handshakes, the great Italian artist left Paris loaded with honors and money and nothing more was done with his plans.

The Colonnade as we know it today resulted from a collaboration between Le Vau, Lemercier, and Perrault. But their project was long in coming. Shortly after work began in 1667, Louis XIV ordered the Colonnade lengthened, a change so basic that it set in motion a domino effect of changes that dragged the work out for years. Then in 1678 the king tired of the Louvre and moved the entire court to Versailles. This brought all work to a halt. The Colonnade had no roof and was detached from the wings at both ends. Portions of the Cour Carrée were still unfinished. Left in this state of abandonment the Louvre became a city within a city. Its spacious rooms filled with squatters made up of courtesans, artisans, artists, and ne'er-do-wells skirting the law, who subdivided floors both vertically and horizontally to create additional floors and rooms. This improvised population was even catered to by restaurants and cabarets that set up in the Louvre as

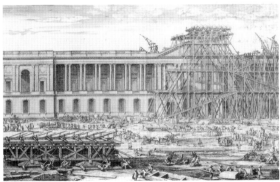

well. Outside, the Cour Carrée became crowded with hastily built houses.

In 1756, under Louis XV, the Louvre's residents were expelled and all extraneous structures were torn down. Construction resumed and was only completed during the First Empire. The Cour Carrée was finished in 1810, and the Colonnade in 1811, almost 150 years after the project had begun.

▲▲ The Louvre in the 17th century, seen from the Left Bank, a hodgepodge of styles with the medieval tower from Philippe-Auguste's fortress on the right and a Renaissance pavilion on the left. (engraving, Israël Sylvestre; Musée Carnavalet, ©PMVP/Negative Degraces)

▲ The Colonnade of the Louvre under construction in 1677. (engraving, Sebastien Leclerc)

⑪ Cour Napoléon, Site of I. M. Pei's Pyramid

Walk through the arch towards the pyramid. Stop at the top of the stairs.

Today the Louvre has a shape resembling that of a horseshoe. But for many years it was rectangular in shape, closed on all sides. See the engraving on p. 118. The wing that no longer exists connected the two long wings of the Louvre and was known as the Palais des Tuileries.

After the accidental death of Henri II in a jousting accident in 1559, a distraught Catherine de Médicis fled her palace in the Marais and took up residence in the Louvre. In 1564, she decided to build her own palace a few hundred yards to the west of the Louvre on the other side of the Charles V wall. This, the Palais des Tuileries, designed by Philibert Delorme, was still under construction in 1572, when Catherine de Médicis's Italian astrologer, Cosimo Ruggieri, made the devastating prediction that she "would die near St. Germain." Her new Palais des Tuileries was in the parish of Saint-Germain l'Auxerrois. Frightened by this prognostication, she left her unfinished Tuileries and

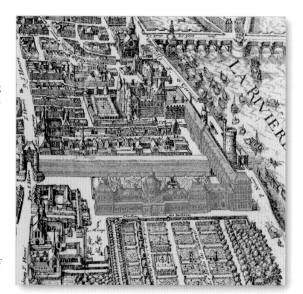

◀ In blue, the Palais des Tuileries of Catherine de Médicis, situated parallel to the wall of Charles V, in yellow. Note that the palace here is at right angles to the Grande Galerie, in red. This is not true to the actual site. (Merian map, 1615)

▶ The Cour Carrée is complete. The Charles V wall is gone but the multitude of houses and ancient streets remain between the two palaces. It was left to Haussmann to clear these. Note the lack of right angle between the Palais des Tuileries and the Grande Galerie. This is true to the actual site. (Turgot map, 1739)

▲ Palais des Tuileries. The small arch, l'Arc du Carrousel, still stands, but with the palace behind it gone and a garden in place today, the site bears no resemblance to its former design. The arch was constructed by Percier and Fontaine for Napoléon I between 1806 and 1808.

built another royal residence in today's Les Halles quarter. While in Blois in 1588, she was taken deathly ill. A priest was called to perform the last rites. Catherine asked the man his name. He replied, "I am Julien de Saint-Germain." She died less than a month later.

While still at the Palais des Tuileries, Catherine conceived the idea of connecting her palace to the Louvre with a long corridor, an idea to be realized by her son-in-law Henri IV. And today we have the Grande Galerie stretching along the Seine a full 1,450 feet, or over four football fields in length. Work on the Grande Galerie was begun in 1595 and completed in 1608, two years before Henri IV's assassination.

Look at a map of Paris and

▲ These buildings stood in the middle of the Place du Carrousel until Haussmann demolished them in the mid-19th century. In the foreground, the Hôtel de Nantes. On the left, a portion of the north wing of the Louvre along Rue de Rivoli.

notice that the Grande Galerie is not on the same plane as the Cour Carrée, but stands closer to the Seine. This was not an aesthetic choice but rather a matter of practicality. Construction of the Grande Galerie would be faster and more economical, it was reasoned, if it was built upon the old foundations of Charles V's wall that ran along the Seine. By the 1860s, these foundations demonstrated such signs of failure that the section between the large arches on the Seine and the Pavillon de Flore at the western end of the Galerie was torn down and rebuilt.

Napoléon I began construction of the north wing of the Louvre along the Rue de Rivoli in 1810, based on designs by Percier and Fontaine. But he completed only a small portion of this wing; the rest was left to Haussmann. In 1857, working with architects Ludovic Visconti and Lefeul, he

accomplished something that generations of French rulers had dreamt of.

The construction of the northern wing of the Louvre brought to the fore a problem that had long preoccupied architects of the Louvre. Any map of Paris clearly shows that the Grande Galerie and the north wing of the Louvre are not parallel. The reason for this, something few people today would know, is that Catherine de Médicis' Palais

▲▲ A section of the Grande Galerie in demolition because of faulty foundations. Reconstruction was carried out between 1861 and 1865. On the right, the southern section of the Palais des Tuileries. (from *The Paris of Henri IV*, Hilary Ballon; ©BHVP/Negative Leyris)

▲ Project for the completion of the Louvre by Ludovic Visconti. 1853. (from *The Paris of Henri IV*, Hilary Ballon; ©BHVP/Negative Leyris)

des Tuileries was constructed parallel to the Charles V wall, which stood not at right angles to the Seine but rather at a slight angle to the river. When Napoléon I began the north wing he had a choice to make: Lay this wing out at right angles to the Palais des Tuileries or parallel to the Grande Galerie. He chose the former.

This lack of parallel between the two wings of the Louvre rankled Haussmann to no end. Napoléon I was not so troubled. "Only birds notice the irregularity of grand spaces," he said. Haussmann, however, found this misalignment so bothersome that he built the two wings that extend out from the Cour Carrée to hide this affront. They are perfectly parallel.

What an irony that Catherine de Médicis' Palais des Tuileries was destroyed during the uprising of the 1871 Commune. The only silver lining to this disaster is the

spectacular vista that opened up from the Louvre to the Arc de Triomphe, one of the most exciting vistas in any city in the world. How unfortunate that it was compromised by the construction of La Défense in the 1970s.

▲▲ The Cour Napoléon seen from Place du Carrousel.

▲ Pavillon Denon in the Cour Napoléon.

⑫ Avenue de l'Opéra

Leave the Cour Napoleon and I. M. Pei's pyramid and walk towards Rue de Rivoli. Cross the street and proceed to Place André Malraux at the beginning of the Avenue de l'Opéra.

▲ The Opéra Garnier is complete. This scene, calm around 1900, is today a frenzy of cars, buses, and crowds. There is a large Métro entrance on this square in front of the opera house.

On your way to Place André Malraux you will pass Place Colette. By all means avoid looking at the new Métro entrance next to the news kiosk. Colette is likely turning in her grave.

Look up the Avenue de l'Opéra to the first row of buildings on the left between the Place Colette and Rue de l'Echelle. Walk over there. This spot corresponds roughly to the top photo on the opposite page. The Avenue de l'Opéra was originally named Avenue Napoléon and was given its present name in 1873 after Napoléon III had gone into exile. Conceived in 1854, long before the opera house, the new avenue was created as a link between the Louvre and

the Grands Boulevards, as well as to give the Left Bank easier access to the Right Bank, then the commercial center of Paris.

To create this avenue, Haussmann had to level a small hill that stood between Place André Malraux and Rue des Pyramides. This hill, la Butte des Moulins (Windmill Hill), was just outside of Paris, and in the 15th century stood on the other side of Charles V's wall.

In September 1429, Paris was occupied by the English. A young Joan of Arc stood on this very hill, along with an army of over twelve thousand, and prepared to deliver Paris from the English by taking the grand entry that stood here, the Porte Saint-Honoré. Surprised by the size of

the moat surrounding the fortification, she was measuring the depth of the water with a rod when she was shot in the calf with an arrow. As the name implies, the hill was covered with windmills. It was also the place where criminals met their punishment—in public, as was the custom then. Counterfeiters were boiled alive in oil. Other criminals were boiled in water.

The building of the Avenue de l'Opéra took place in stages. The north section, between Rue Louis le Grand and Boulevard des Capucines, was completed in 1864, and the south end, between today's Place André Malraux and Rue de l'Echelle, in 1868. Nine years later, with scaffolding

▲ Windmill Hill—la Butte des Moulins—is being leveled. The beginning of Avenue de l'Opéra on the left is already in place with all of Haussmann's accoutrements, e.g., building, wide sidewalk, street lamp, trees. Garnier argued that trees spoiled the view of his opera house and had them removed.

► Same view today. The building on the left is the same as in the photo above. Compare the balcony in both photos.

still standing where buildings were yet to rise, General Mac Mahon, President of the Republic, with great ceremony, led an inaugural parade down the new avenue.

Electric light was used during construction of the avenue, but it was years before this invention was offered to the public. Many people thought it was too harsh on the eyes. The only people who will profit, it was said, were the oculists. Work on the avenue stopped because of the devastating Franco-Prussian war and then the Commune. Finally completed, the avenue was slow to find favor with the public. It did not reach its full popularity until the Universal Exposition of 1900.

▲ View from the top of the opera house, circa 1870. Only the top of the new avenue is complete here. (photo, Marville; Musée Carnavalet, ©PMVP/Negative Leyris)

⑬ Galerie d'Orléans in the Palais Royal

Cross the Avenue de l'Opéra, Rue de Richelieu, and Rue Montpensier to enter the Galerie d'Orléans.

▶ Galerie de Bois, closing the Palais Royal garden on the south side.

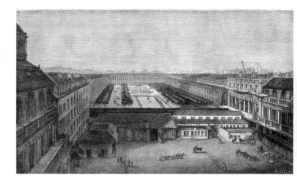

This site, innocuous enough today, is holy ground for any architect. The concept of the covered passage, a most pleasant urban experience in many quarters of the world, was conceived here. The first passage, the Galerie de Bois, constructed on this spot in 1786, was built entirely of wood, and was a new urban experience—a protected environment filled with shops offering the finest luxury articles, safe from the harsh weather, noise, filth, and jostling of the streets. In effect, this was an early version of the shopping mall. The passage was enormously successful and led to its extension in 1790 with the Galerie Vitrée, the first glass-covered passage in Paris, situated at right angles to the Galerie de Bois.

In 1827, the Galerie Vitrée went up in flames. The Galerie de Bois escaped the inferno, but because of its vulnerability to fire was torn down along with the remains of the Galerie Vitrée. Construction on a new Galerie d'Orléans began immediately with more durable materials of stone and marble and was completed in 1829. This *galerie* stood until 1935. The success of the covered passageway in the Palais Royal created a vogue in Paris, with the construction of over fifty passageways, most located on the Right Bank. Today, no more than fifteen remain.

▲▲ Galerie Vitrée on the left and right adjoining the Galerie de Bois. (Musée Carnavalet, ©PMVP)

▲ Galerie d'Orléans at the height of its popularity, before the rise of the department store eclipsed the passages.

▲ Galerie d'Orléans, topped by a skylight, enclosing the Palais Royal garden.

▲ Site of the Galerie d'Orléans today. Nothing remains except the rows of columns. Match the columns in the distance with the columns at the end of the passageway in the engraving on the left. (photo, K. Leimkuhler)

⑭ The Palais Royal Garden

Enter the garden.

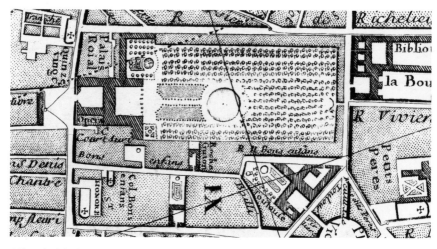

▲ The garden before it was enclosed by the Duke of Orléans in 1786. The Seine is to the left. (Delagrive map; ©BHVP/Negative Leyris)

All those who enjoy the Palais Royal garden today owe a debt of gratitude to the most base human traits of wantonness and debauchery.

Explanation: The Palais Royal was built by Cardinal Richelieu between 1629 and 1636. By 1781 the site was in the hands of Louis XIV's great-grandson, the fifth Duke of Orléans. The site then was classic in its design: a palace with a large garden behind. The Duke, a great libertine, led a life of extravagance far beyond his means and found himself on the brink of ruin. An entrepreneurial friend had an idea: Enclose the garden with shops on the ground level and apartments above. Income! This was a novel idea—a member of the royalty engaging in commerce was unheard of. The architect, Victor Louis, drew up plans

and construction began. By 1786 the garden had been enclosed on three sides. Foundations for the south side had been laid but the Duke's finances were exhausted. Louis suggested that the Duke throw up something temporary as a measure to protect these foundations while the Duke waited for his money to accrue. This was the famous Galerie de Bois.

The new Palais Royal became the most popular attraction in Paris and exceeded the Duke's expectations. Crowds flocked day and night to indulge every taste and fancy in an atmosphere as lively as a Middle Eastern bazaar. If Paris was the center of France, the Palais Royal was the center of Paris. Everything could be found there: in the cafés with their fine wines, beers, coffees, and chocolate; in the

restaurants with their haute cuisine; or in the elegant shops with the finest clothes, jewelry, glass, porcelain, and clocks. Given the absence of local police, who were forbidden to enter royal grounds, the Palais Royal had the additional feature of numerous gaming tables and brothels, which only added to its notoriety.

The Palais Royal's reputation became known around the world and made it a must-see for anyone visiting Paris. An Englishman captured the attraction of the garden when he wrote, "Contemplated by the eye of reason, the Palais Royal exhibits a sink of dissipation, a vortex of profligacy, an abyss of vice, of ruin and corruption. As a curiosity it unquestionably merits to be seen."

Cafés were very partisan places in those days. The

▲ 19th-century strollers under the arcades.

▲ Galerie de Beaujolais. The restaurant Grand Véfour is one of the oldest restaurants in Paris, dating from the 1780s.

prostitutes found camaraderie at Café de la Renommée. Financiers and lawyers went to the Café de Foy (57–60 Galerie de Montpensier), which also had the tastiest sorbet. The best chocolate was found at Café Lemblin (100–102 Galerie de Beaujolais), where philosophers, composers, and writers met. The Café des Aveugles (Café of the Blind) was in the cellar below Café Lemblin, and during the Revolution was home to the sans-culottes. Entertainment was provided by an orchestra of four blind musicians. The Café des Mille Colonnes (36 Galerie de Montpensier) was run by a proprietor renowned for her low-cut dresses. The mirrored

walls reflected the café's interior to infinity, thus providing its name (Café of a Thousand Columns).

The grand vogue of the Palais Royal eventually passed. The closing of the brothels in 1831 and the gaming tables in 1836, plus the ascent of the Grands Boulevards as *the* place to be in Paris, all contributed to its demise.

The only vestige of the garden's past glory today is the restaurant Grand Véfour. During the Revolution the popular actress Mlle. Montansier lived in an apartment above the restaurant. In a single evening she entertained a group comprised of Robespierre, Hébert,

Jean-Paul Marat, Danton, and the Duke of Orléans. *Quelle soirée!* Little did the Duke know that among the guests that evening were those who would send him to the guillotine in November 1793. Nor could he know that they would follow.

By the mid-19th century the Palais Royal was deserted. A writer in 1911 described the site as "a thing of the past . . . never likely to awake." It was only as recently as the 1980s that the garden began to fill again with adoring crowds. Restaurants have opened under the arcades, with tables spilling out into the garden, bringing life and animation back to this urban treasure.

▲ A proposal by Eugène Hénard to bisect the Palais Royal garden with a roadway, part of a larger east–west thoroughfare cutting across Paris, 1904. (from *Etudes sur les transformations de Paris*, 1903–1909, Eugène Hénard; ©BHVP/Negative Leyris)

▲ The Palais Royal garden today.

▲ This large structure in the middle of the garden was built in 1786 to replace the Paris opera house, which had burned down. Sunken fifteen feet belowground and rising ten feet aboveground, this curious hall was called "Le Cirque" and was used for equestrian presentations. It did not last long: It was lost in a fire in 1798. In the distance, the Galerie de Bois. (reconstruction by Hoffbauer)

15 Covered Passages Vivienne and Colbert

Exit the Palais Royal by the Galerie de Beaujolais. Across the street, to the right of Rue Vivienne, are stairs leading through a short, narrow passageway. This leads to Rue des Petits Champs. Across the street are Galerie Vivienne and Galerie Colbert.

The Galerie Vivienne was built in 1826 from a design by F. J. Delannoy during the great vogue of the covered passages. The success of this passage inspired developers to build the Galerie Colbert next door. If location is everything in business, this location could not have been better. The developers had every reason to expect their passage, in the center of Paris, in a prosperous quarter near the Palais Royal and the Galerie Vivienne, with constant foot traffic, to rival its neighbors, but this was not the case. Not in the 19th, 20th, or 21st century.

At its inauguration in September 1827, the Galerie Colbert was praised for its elegant design. Noteworthy was its large domed rotunda. Beneath this glass dome

stood a magnificent bronze candelabra with seven crystal globes, which became a popular point of rendezvous for gentlemen meeting young ladies. Architects from around Europe studied the gallery's design closely. Among them was the Italian Mengoni, who drew inspiration for his monumental Galleria Vittorio Emanuele II in Milan. But for all its attractions the Colbert never rose to the level of the Vivienne in its appreciation by the public.

By the mid-19th century it made no difference. The invention of the department store, with an intoxicating array of luxury items, plus Haussmann's broad new thoroughfares free of open sewers, signaled the demise

of the passages. Light, sunshine, and air, heralded by Haussmann as the raison d'etre for his demolitions, became part of a new health code that made the enclosed passageways not only out of fashion but for many, unhealthy. By the end of the century the passageways were totally eclipsed, viewed by the public as no more than "umbrellas for the poor." The Galerie Colbert became a no-man's-land, to the point that it was closed in 1975. It was only saved from demolition after being purchased by the Bibliothèque Nationale, which occupies the site today. The *galerie* reopened in 1986, completely restored, but to this day remains in the shadow of its neighbor, Vivienne.

◀▶ Galerie Vivienne today. Though less frequented than in its glory days in the 19th century, it remains one of the most pleasant spots in Paris.

▲ Glass rotunda of the Galerie Colbert, inaugurated in 1827.

▲ Galerie Colbert. This rotunda was closely studied as a model for the giant passage in Milan, the Galleria Vittorio Emanuele II.

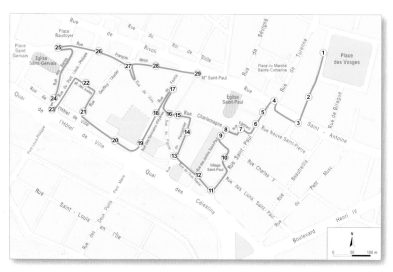

▲ Itinerary.

▲ 6 Rue Beautreillis. The last vestige of the Hôtel Raoul, demolished in 1965.

The Marais

Starting point:	Place des Vosges
Métro:	Saint-Paul, Bastille, or Chemin Vert
Length of walk:	Approximately 3 hours

This walk begins in the Place des Vosges, the centerpiece of the Marais and one of the jewels of Paris. From here you will walk through the neighboring Hôtel de Sully, and then across Rue Saint-Antoine to the south Marais quarters of Saint-Paul and Saint-Gervais.

Most of this walk tells the story of titanic battles waged in this quarter from the 1930s to the 1960s between powerful city bureaucracies intent on massive demolition and individuals fighting to save the Marais from oblivion. Much of the stroller's experience in this quarter today results from decisions made during that period of the 20th century.

The Marais reached the height of its splendor in the 17th century when it was the aristocratic quarter of Paris. The construction of Place des Vosges, plus the numerous town houses that went up in the quarter sparing nothing in their magnificence, gave the Marais an elegance without rival in the city. But fashions change, and by the early 18th century the upper classes began moving to newer, more elegant houses in the Saint-Germain quarter. And with this the Marais began a slow descent into oblivion. The Revolution of 1789 emptied the quarter of the nobility and opened the doors to a population of petite bourgeoisie, people who actually worked for a living. Lacking an endless source of income to maintain the quarter, the Marais' elegance wore thin. The Industrial Revolution brought tens of thousands of people seeking work to the capital, and many landed in the Marais. This formerly aristocratic area became a working-class neighborhood where upkeep was a low priority.

By the early 1900s waves of Jewish immigrants fleeing Eastern Europe had settled here to eke out a living. Landlords profited from the influx by sub-dividing spacious apartments into smaller ones, or dividing rooms horizontally to create a second floor. Courtyards were enclosed under tin and glass roofs to create work space for the numerous cottage industries that sprang up. Buildings crept higher as additional floors were added on top. Masses of people worked, slept, and ate in cramped, unhealthy spaces where air and light were precious commodities. By the 1950s the quarter had attained the desperate status of a slum. The solution proposed by the city was to carry out massive demolition in the clear-cutting style of urbanism popular at the time.

As news of the city's plans became known, a great struggle ensued. A city bureaucracy with notions of modernism laced with a disdain for all things old squared off against the preservationists armed with an intimate knowledge of the quarter's history and a deep appreciation for the beauty of its architecture. They argued for restoration rather than demolition.

Protesters found their voice in Michel Raude. If there is a single individual deserving credit for saving the Marais, it is he. In 1962 Raude created the Festival du Marais, a summer-long extravaganza of world-class theatre and dance concerts performed inside the very mansions being threatened with destruction. Thousands of Parisians who had turned their backs on the Marais flocked to these performances and found a renewed appreciation for this old and battered quarter. This did much to mobilize public opinion. The Minister of Culture, André Malraux, was slow to warm to the idea of saving the Marais, but under the influence of Finance Minister Michel Debré, as well as rising pressure from the Parisian public, he finally came to embrace the effort. In August 1962 he created the now-famous Malraux Law, declaring the entire Marais a "safeguarded sector"—in effect placing a prohibition on demolition of any kind. The city stepped in with an array of financial incentives to encourage property owners to restore their buildings to their original state. The success of this initiative is obvious. A former slum is now some of the most expensive real estate in Paris.

What would the Marais look like today had an enlightened few not fought for its resurrection? For the answer, walk over to 6 Rue Beautreillis to see the mutilated remains of an 18th-century mansion, the Hôtel Raoul, demolished in 1965. The *hôtel's* stately coach entrance stands isolated before a modern apartment building whose mediocrity would hold up to the best public housing projects in any American city. Amputated, this architectural remnant now suffers the final indignity of being left to disintegrate under the elements.

▶ Place des Vosges.

① Place des Vosges

Stand on the west side of the square in front of number 15.

▲ The jousting tournament held in 1559 in the Hôtel des Tournelles in which Henri II was fatally wounded.

The Place des Vosges was built by Henri IV between 1605 and 1612, and as Victor Hugo observed, is the result of an unfortunate accident—a poke in the eye. In the 16th century the royal palace known as the Hôtel des Tournelles stood on this site. In 1559, Henri II and his wife Catherine de Médicis threw a celebration here in honor of their daughter Elizabeth's marriage to King Phillip II of Spain. The king, a true sporting type, organized a jousting tournament to close the celebration. For his opponent he invited Captain Gabriel Montgomery of the King's Scottish Guards. Montgomery at first declined, but the king insisted. Suited up in their armor and with lances poised, they mounted their steeds and charged.

Unfortunately Montgomery's lance knocked open the king's visor and pierced him in the eye. The king languished for ten days and died. The distraught queen ordered the palace torn down and fled to the Louvre where she took up royal residence.

For nearly fifty years the site of the old palace stood empty, serving at times as a market for horse traders or a place where duelists settled scores. Then in 1605 Henri IV announced the creation of the Place Royale, a new public square, to stimulate French trade and commerce. On the north side of the square he would build a factory for the manufacture of fine silk fabric to rival the imported Italian silk then popular with the French nobility. The other three sides of the square

would consist of apartments to provide lodging for artisans, merchants, and tradespeople. The ground level would be designed with covered arcades lined with shops selling a wide variety of luxury items.

When the silk-making enterprise failed in 1607, the king demolished the factory and in its place built a row of houses matching the other three sides of the square. The square was inaugurated in April 1612 as Place Royale and became home to Paris' circle of nobility. Strutting on this royal stage became an art form in itself as aristocrats, wrapped in powdered wigs and ruffles, in fine brocaded attire, paraded across the expanse of lawn or under the arcades past the elegant shops of fine linen, lace, gold, silver, and armor.

► Place des Vosges (numbers 22 and 24) in the 1940s.

▲ Place Royale in the 17th century. (engraving, Aveline; Musée Carnavalet, ©PMVP/Negative Ladet)

◄ ▼ ▼ The Place des Vosges was almost entirely renovated during the 1960s and 1970s. Numbers 15 and 20 received their face lift as late as 2001. Number 2 is the last holdout. Directly below and to the left, the courtyard and staircase of number 15.

The fortunes of the square, now called Place des Vosges, declined over the years along with the rest of the Marais, and for the same reasons. Changing fashion, the influx of poor populations, and lack of maintenance took their toll. By 1900 this once-glorious site was described as "somber as a prison . . . its doors look lifeless . . . the stones are black, the arches cracked . . . it looks sick and tired." Today, after years of renovation, it sparkles once again.

② Hôtel de Sully

Walk under the arcade, following the apartment numbers as they descend until you reach the corner. There you will find a small arched doorway leading into an adjoining garden. Enter there.

This is the garden of the Hôtel de Sully. The *hôtel* was designed by Jean Androuet du Cerceau, built between 1624 and 1630, and named after the Duke of Sully, minister of Henri IV, who acquired the residence about four years after its completion. The wealth and splendor of the Marais in the 17th century is apparent. Notice the decorative sculptures on the facade facing the garden. Today, the Hôtel de Sully houses the Centre des Monuments Nationaux. Along with many activities centered on historic preservation, it offers fine photo exhibits in a wing in the garden. As you walk through the short passage leading in the direction of Rue Saint-Antoine, notice the fine sculpted ceiling overhead. On your right is a large bookstore specializing in French heritage, well worth a visit.

Continue into the courtyard and notice the figures on the

▲ The Orangerie in the garden of the Hôtel de Sully.

▼ Courtyard of the Hôtel de Sully.

facades representing the four elements, Air, Earth, Fire, and Water, and the four seasons. Exit through the large archway onto Rue Saint-Antoine.

▶ Detail of the facade of the courtyard above. On left, Autumn. On right, Winter.

Rue Saint-Antoine ③

Exit the Hôtel de Sully and cross Rue Saint-Antoine to view the building's facade.

Rue Saint-Antoine is one of the oldest roads in Paris, dating back to Roman times. To trace its history is to trace the history of France: from medieval days when small communities of peasants lived here on what was then the edge of the city, to the pomp and pageantry of the 17th century when this was the most fashionable quarter in Paris, to the rebellious days of the 19th century when the Rue Saint-Antoine was the scene of bloody uprisings.

The Hôtel de Sully came into the hands of the State in 1944 and has undergone a full restoration. During work on the site a perfectly preserved 17th-century hand-painted ceiling was discovered behind a lower false ceiling, put in place perhaps to hold the heat in colder months.

Compare today's building with the postcard image in the middle of this page. In 1796 the Hôtel de Sully was acquired by a Monsieur Dupré, who quickly converted it into a pure profit venture. The empty space between the two second-story wings was filled in, altering the front elevation, and the ground floor was opened up to the street in order to create commercial space. To the right of the main entrance in the postcard is a shoe store, Chaussures Incroyable. On the left, a bank, Credit Lyonnais. Balconies were added to the facade in the 18th century. These were removed in the renovation. The Hôtel de Sully exemplifies the fate of many classic buildings in the Marais when their value was measured only in terms of profit.

▲▲▲ Rue Saint-Antoine, circa 1900. On the right in the distance, the Hôtel de Sully.

▲▲ Hôtel de Sully severely modified to increase its commercial value.

▲ Hôtel de Sully fully restored.

④ **Rue de Turenne**

Follow Rue Saint-Antoine to Rue de Turenne.

Rue de Turenne was widened in 1877. To see something most unusual, cross Rue Saint-Antoine to Rue de Turenne and notice the long wall running along the street with the small patch of grass in front. This wall is the interior of the building that was torn down for the street widening. Look carefully at ground level and if the grass is not too high you will see the outline of a stairway in the wall. At the second-story level you can see the hallway with the painted letters 1ᴱᴿᴱ ETAGE (first floor) and, a few feet to the right, CONCIERGE ADROITE (concierge to the right).

▶ Rue de Turenne seen from Rue Saint-Antoine. Both these buildings were demolished for street widening in 1877. (photo, Godefroy)

◀ Same view today.

▲ Rue de Turenne. A wall reveals traces of the building that was lost during street widening.

Rue Saint-Paul ⑤

Cross Rue Saint-Antoine and walk to Rue Saint-Paul.

▶ 47 Rue Saint-Paul before restoration.
(photo, l'Association pour la Sauvegarde
et Mise en Valeur du Paris Historique)

▶▶ Same building today.

At 47 Rue Saint-Paul is
a tall, narrow building
dating from 1545 known as the
Silver Tower (Tour d'Argent).
The city bought the building
in 1964 and immediately
slapped a demolition
permit on it because of its
dilapidated condition. In its
place something thoroughly
mediocre would have certainly
been constructed. But a
neighborhood organization,
l'Association pour la
Sauvegarde et Mise en Valeur
du Paris Historique, stepped in
and guaranteed to restore the
building to its original state.
The city relented. Renovation
was carried out between 1968
and 1971 with all volunteer
labor. A building of similar
vintage to the left, at number
49, was not so lucky.

◀ The cinema Saint-Paul, circa 1940.
Demolished in 1966–67.

▶ Same view today.

6 Rue Neuve Saint-Pierre

Cross the street and stand in front of 41 Rue Saint-Paul.

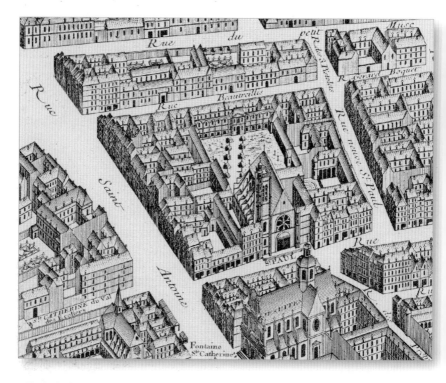

▲ The Church of Saint-Paul des Champs, built in 1431, stands on Rue Saint-Paul. To the left is the large tower, a remnant of which remains today. See photo on next page. (Turgot map detail)

Rue Neuve Saint-Pierre is a recent addition to Paris, having been created in 1913. The photo at the top of the facing page shows one of the buildings (17th century) among those demolished. The arch on the right led into Passage Saint-Paul, which in turn led into an ancient cemetery attached to the Church of Saint-Paul des Champs. Built in 1431, the church (visible in the Turgot map above) served as a meeting hall during the Revolution, as well as a depot for royal carriages brought to Paris from Versailles where they were stripped of their gold and steel. The facade featured a stained glass window created in 1436 depicting Joan of Arc. The church was nationalized during the Revolution and demolished in 1793.

Notice the tower to the left of the church in the Turgot map and what appears to be a garden behind it. That is the cemetery mentioned above. It was in use for over a thousand years, from the 7th century until the Revolution. It is said that Rabelais was buried there.

A vestige of this medieval church survives. On the corner of Rue Neuve Saint-Pierre and Rue Saint-Paul stands a small one-story shop. Look through the window on the Rue Saint-Paul side, and in the corner near the window you can see a remnant of the old church tower—the bottom step of a staircase that led to the top of the tower. This is one of many instances in Paris of ancient architectural remnants incorporated into modern buildings.

▲ 32–34 Rue Saint-Paul in October 1913, a month before demolition. The arch leads into Passage Saint-Paul. (photo, Berthaud)

◀ Passage Saint-Paul. The buildings at the end of the passage open onto Rue Saint-Paul. (photo, Godefroy)

▲ Rue Neuve Saint-Pierre, created in 1913.

▶ Demolition of Passage Saint-Paul for Rue Neuve Saint-Pierre. On the right, Rue Saint-Paul. Vestiges of the old tower, for years hidden by newer buildings, are revealed here. The section in blue can be seen today in the window of the small shop on the corner.

⑦ Rue Eginhard

Cross Rue Saint-Paul and enter Rue Eginhard at 31 Rue Saint-Paul. Follow this tiny street to Rue Charlemagne and then do an about-face.

▲ Rue Saint-Paul. At the extreme left is the entrance to Rue Eginhard.

▲ Rue Eginhard circa 1900.

▲ Plaque commemorating the Zadjner family, apprehended by the French, deported by the Nazis.

▲ Same view today. These photos give a good feel for the shabbiness of the neighborhood when it was still a poor Jewish ghetto, Le Pletzl, lived in by immigrants scraping by.

Rue Eginhard is so short that "street" seems somewhat of a misnomer. Perhaps "passage" is more appropriate. It was originally property of the religious order Dames Hospitalières de Sainte-Anastasie. In 1648 a young prioress undertook to build seven houses on this street in order to enrich the coffers of her religious order. Construction was completed in 1666. Of the original seven houses, only two remain.

Notice the plaque on the stone pedestal. A building once stood on the same patch of grass. The plaque commemorates the Zadjner family and tells a tragic story, not only of the Zadjners, but of the whole quarter. The plaque reads, "Here lived Monsieur Elias Zadjner. Died for France at the age of 41. Former resistance fighter deported to Auschwitz in May 1944 with his three sons, Albert age 21, Salomon and Bernard age 15.

They died in the unit of medical experiments. We shall never forget."

The Zadjners came to Paris in 1934 from Poland. During the Jewish deportations carried out by the French during the Nazi occupation of World War II, the family played a game of cat and mouse, moving from one house to another in order to avoid the deadly sweeps.

On May 1, 1944, the family was at home waiting for Catholic priests who were

▲ Rue Eginhard in the 1940s. The building at the end of the street was demolished in 1962.

◀ Rue Eginhard after renovation.

▶ Corner of Rue Charlemagne and Rue Eginhard, circa 1940.

◄ Same view after restoration. The wooden storefronts have been removed, revealing the original stone facades.

to take the Zadjner twins, Salomon and Bernard, into hiding in the countryside. There was a knock at the door. It was not the priests, but the French police, acting on behalf of the Nazis. Deportation! The family scrambled. One of the boys, Joseph, and his mother managed to get away. Daughter Sarah tried to escape across the roof but was caught along with her three brothers and father. They were all deported. Sarah was the sole survivor.

In 1995 a ceremony was held in this quarter to mark the 50th anniversary of the liberation of Auschwitz. Among the attendees was Mayor Jacques Chirac. Sarah Zadjner approached the mayor and told him her story, and how for 50 years she has appealed to the city for a plaque to be installed on the spot where her family lived. A month later, authorization was granted.

Truthfully speaking, there should be plaques throughout the neighborhood for all the Jews who were deported to the camps. For this building alone you would see plaques for Laja and Zysla Jankielewicz; Isidore and Anna Bilcorai; Rachel and Idel Pollac; Ben

Schlachter, a Russian from Riga; and Maurice Norynberg, the shoemaker.

At the very end of the street, on the left, notice the round window with the 17th-century wrought iron monogram of the initials S. A. for Sainte-Anastasie.

⑧ **Rue Charlemagne**

Follow Rue Charlemagne to Rue des Jardins Saint-Paul, then do an about-face.

Several of the houses you walked by are of recent construction. Number 8, on your left, dates from 1978 and houses a day-care center. The fountain on the left, in place since 1840, provides water from the Canal de l'Ourcq.

► Corner of Rue Charlemagne and Rue des Jardins Saint-Paul around 1940. The building on the left was torn down in the 1970s. The corner building on the right is clearly visible today. Had post-war renovation plans been carried out, this building and everything else in this neighborhood would have been demolished.

◄ Same view today. Compare building on right corner with same in photos on facing page.

▲ View of Rue Charlemagne and Rue des Jardins Saint-Paul.

► Same view today after renovation.

9 Rue des Jardins Saint-Paul

▲ Rue des Jardins Saint-Paul. View towards the Seine, July 1942.   ▲ Same view in September 1948. The houses have been demolished, revealing the wall of Philippe-Auguste on the right.

Until the mid-1940s the large playfield before you, part of the adjacent Lycée Charlemagne, was covered with houses. The demolition of these buildings revealed the largest remaining section of Philippe-Auguste's wall, built between 1190 and 1210. Had you been standing on this spot in the early 13th century you would have been outside of Paris. This narrow street has been called Rue des Jardins Saint-Paul since 1277, most likely because at the time Parisians were cultivating fields along this part of the wall. The tower standing on Rue Charlemagne is where Montgomery was briefly incarcerated after his tragic jousting accident with Henri II in 1559.

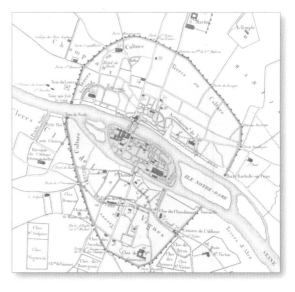

▲ Wall of Philippe-Auguste. The blue patch on the right corresponds to the wall remnant on Rue des Jardins Saint-Paul.

▲ View of the wall of Philippe-Auguste.

► Rue des Jardins Saint-Paul in 1899. The houses on the left were torn down in 1944–46. (photo, Atget)

▼ Rue des Jardins Saint-Paul today. At the end of the street is the fountain providing water from the Canal de l'Ourcq.

10 Village Saint-Paul

From Rue des Jardins Saint-Paul walk through one of the arches leading into Village Saint-Paul.

The Village Saint-Paul consists of about fifty buildings dating from the 17th and 18th centuries. By the early 1970s they were in such a decrepit condition that the city had them slated for demolition. The condition of some apartments was so deplorable that they had to be vacated for health and safety reasons. Less than half of the apartments had running water. Less than 10 percent had individual toilets, and most tenants had to share bathrooms in the hallway. But fashion in urban planning changes like the color of men's ties, and in 1972 the decision was taken to renovate the entire site.

Under the direction of architect Paul Gattier, the number of apartments was reduced from 730 to 241, and the size of the apartments was more than doubled from an average of twenty-three square meters to fifty-eight square meters. Today the city still maintains ownership of the buildings and rents the apartments to the elderly at below market rate.

The Village Saint-Paul is a clear victory of preservation over demolition, yet in its present state it falls seriously short of the success it could achieve. While the courtyards are a pleasant respite from the street, clearly little thought has been given to what might enhance the stroller's experience here. The trees stand in small, doleful plots of earth bordered by mundane metallic fences.

▲ Village Saint-Paul before and after restoration. (*Paris-Projet*, no. 23–24; ©BHVP/ Negative Leyris)

▲ Village Saint-Paul in the early stages of its renovation.

The feeling of potential here is palpable and the mind reels at the possibilities of turning the Village Saint-Paul into a truly idyllic spot in the heart of Paris. The association of businesses in the Village is aware of this problem and is searching for a solution. We wish them spectacular luck.

▼ ► One of several antique shops in Village Saint-Paul.

► Arch leading to Rue Saint-Paul.

► Passage leading to Rue des Jardins Saint-Paul.

⑪ Rue Saint-Paul to Rue de l'Ave Maria

Exit Village Saint-Paul onto Rue Saint-Paul. Turn right, walk to Rue des Lions Saint-Paul, and the to Rue de l'Ave Maria.

◀ Corner of Rue Saint-Paul and Lions Saint-Paul. The tower remains today but the Hotel de la Vieuville on the right has been demolished. (from *Les Vieux Hôtels de Paris*, 10ᵉ série, Contet & Vacqiuer; ©BHVP/Negative Leyris)

▲ Same view today.

Notice the square turret on the corner of the building at the corner of Rue Saint-Paul and Rue des Lions Saint-Paul. This turret dates from the 16th century and is linked to one of the most famous figures in the annals of French crime: la Marquise de Brinvilliers. After eight years of a tepid marriage the Marquise took a lover, a young cavalry officer named Sainte-Croix. When the adulterous couple found themselves in financial straits they devised a plan: Poison the Marquise's husband, father, brothers, and sister and inherit the family fortune. To test the efficacy of her "succession powders" as she called them, the Marquise took a position at the hospital, Hôtel Dieu, as a *dame de charité*, where she used the patients as guinea pigs to determine the correct dosage.

It was in this corner tower, legend has it, that she prepared her concoctions.

The couple's treachery was uncovered one day when Sainte-Croix dropped dead in his Left Bank apartment, apparently asphyxiated by fumes from poisons he was mixing. A box found in his room contained letters from the Marquise detailing their exploits, along with recipes and vials of her chosen poisons. She was beheaded in 1676 on the Place du Grève, today's Place de l'Hôtel de Ville, before a crowd of thousands. Her remains were cremated and her ashes scattered to the winds.

Before going any further, notice the several streets nearby: Rue Beautreillis (beautiful trellis), Rue de la Cerisae (cherry orchard), Rue Charles V, and Rue des Lions

Saint-Paul. Therein lies the history of this quarter. Around 1380 Charles V established a large royal domain here, the Hôtel Saint-Pol, extending from Rue Saint-Antoine to the Seine, and from Rue Saint-Paul to Boulevard Bourdon in the east. The Rue des Lions Saint-Paul refers to the exotic animals kept here by the king.

Look across the street to the modern building on the last block of Rue Saint-Paul. Here is a case of urban vandalism, pure and simple. Many buildings of great beauty have been destroyed in Paris through the years, and often for the most dubious reasons. But the case before you exceeds all others for the simple reason than the perpetrator of this act had such pretense to culture and sophistication.

I speak of Mr. Ernest

▲ Hôtel de la Vieuville seen from the quai.

▲ Courtyard of the Hôtel de la Vieuville, 1907. (photo, Barry; ©BHVP/Negative Leyris)

Cognacq, owner of the department store La Samaritaine. Cognacq and his wife, Louise Jay, were renowned collectors of 18th-century French art and for years maintained a museum filled with their collection on the Boulevard des Capucines. Today their museum is located in a 16th-century building, the Hôtel Donon, in the Marais' Rue Elzévir. Cognacq's sophistication, however, did not stop him from tearing down the magnificent Hôtel de la Vieuville that stood on this spot. And for what reason? To build a warehouse for La Samaritaine. The year was 1927.

The Hôtel de la Vieuville was recognized by many as an architectural gem on a par with the Place des Vosges and the Renaissance Cluny Museum. While it had been added onto and reconfigured over the years, its earliest portions dated back to the late 16th century. Its rooms were full of delicious architectural details, including hand-painted wooden beams with designs of flower wreaths and birds, a Louis XIV wrought iron balcony, and decorative sculptures on the facade.

The Hôtel de la Vieuville was originally a sumptuous town house built for the nobility, but in time became a commercial locale. First, a stagecoach office in 1777, then in 1793 a tobacco factory, and in 1822, of all things, a water purification facility. Water, pumped from the Seine into the *hôtel*, was purified through a series of large charcoal filters and then sold to the public. The Galignani Paris guide of 1867 described this water as "perfectly sweet and wholesome."

The destruction of the Hôtel de la Vieuville is a lesson in how architecture and humanity intersect. A long-time resident of the *hôtel* was Lucien Lambeau, a man who dedicated his entire professional life to the preservation of historic Paris. He knew the Hôtel de la Vieuville so well that he probably could see past inhabitants walking the halls at night. Lambeau continued living in the *hôtel* even after demolition began, right up to the last minute when he was forced to move. He died within a year of a broken heart.

▲ Warehouse for La Samaritaine built in 1927 in place of the old Hôtel de la Vieuville. The building received a complete makeover in 1981.

▲ Handsome building that stood at the corner of Rue Saint-Paul and Rue de l'Ave Maria. Demolished around 1900.

▲ Same view today.

⑫ Corner of Rue de l'Ave Maria and Rue des Jardins Saint-Paul

Follow Rue de l'Ave Maria to the first corner.

▲ 8, 10, 12 Rue de l'Ave Maria in December 1942. Demolished. On the left is Rue des Jardins Saint-Paul.

▼ Same view today.

In 1942, every old building you see on this walk, from Stop #5 on, was photographed by the city because, with few exceptions, they were all to be demolished in a great fiasco of urban planning. More on this later. Many of those photos, which you will see in these pages, show the quarter deserted during the German occupation. By 1942 Jews were barred from restaurants, cafés, and cinemas. They could only shop during prescribed hours of the afternoon. Bicycles and radios were confiscated. Telephones were ordered disconnected. Worse yet, many Jews had already been deported to concentration camps. In better times, this neighborhood, though poor, was a very lively place. While total eradication of the quarter was averted, many old buildings were lost to the pickaxe. What these streets gained in modernity they lost in life. The site before you is an example. This corner has been anesthetized by a policy of misguided urbanism. In *The Death and Life of Great American Cities*, American writer Jane Jacobs calls this "The Great Blight of Dullness." Streets once rich with social life are no longer destinations but have degenerated into corridors, someplace you move through to go somewhere else.

The great playwright Molière lived on this corner in the 17th century at the age of twenty-three. His company,

le Théatre Illustre, performed only steps away at 15 Rue l'Ave Maria in the Jeu de Paume de la Croix Noire, a large tennis court inside a building that was torn down in 1728. He only managed to keep his theatre in business from January to August of 1645, when his creditors caught up with him and had him thrown in jail.

To locate Molière's building, imagine extending the Philippe-Auguste wall across Rue de l'Ave Maria. The Théatre Illustre was adjacent to this spot on the outside of the wall. Today you will find nothing there except a city office building built in 1931. The earlier building that stood here was torn down in 1928, and unfortunately took with it a remnant of the Philippe-Auguste wall.

▶ Corner of Rue de l'Ave Maria (left and right) and Rue des Jardins Saint-Paul, the narrow street beyond the intersection, 1901. (photo, Atget)

◀ Same view today.

⑬ Rue du Figuier

Follow Rue de l'Ave Maria to the Hôtel de Sens.

▲ Hôtel de Sens in the 16th century. Note the decoration over the doorway including shields with coats of arms and fleurs-de-lys. These were hammered and scraped off during the Revolution.

▶ Hôtel de Sens around 1900. The market hall on the left was demolished in 1905. The building on the right was demolished in the 1930s.

The Hôtel de Sens was built by Archbishop Tristan de Salazar between 1498 and 1519, and is one of the last two remaining medieval buildings in Paris. The other is the Cluny Museum on the Left Bank. The *hôtel* was built for the Archbishops of Sens for their frequent visits to Paris, which was then only a diocese subordinate to the archdiocese of Sens. Paris received its own archbishop in 1623, and by 1650 the *hôtel* was in private hands.

Salazar was more of a soldier than an ecclesiastic and only received his position because his father had saved the life of Louis XI. The *hôtel*'s architecture reveals Salazar's military mind, with turrets extending out from the facade in order to better survey the surrounding streets. It is said that the entry arch was designed with the uppermost part extending over the doorway to permit the pouring of boiling oil onto hostiles below.

In 1605, after a long exile from Paris, Marguerite de Valois (Queen Margot), daughter of Henri II of the famous jousting accident, gained permission to live in the Hôtel de Sens. The origin of the street name, Rue du Figuier, derives from a great fig tree that once stood before the entrance to the *hôtel*. Because it encumbered the comings and goings of Margot's carriage, she had it cut down.

But the queen did not live here for long. She had a weakness for young lovers and in May 1606, at age fifty-two, this led to a most dramatic incident. One morning as she entered the Hôtel de Sens accompanied by her twenty-year-old lover, Julian Date, her former lover, the eighteen-year-old Count de Vermond, stepped forward and shot his rival in the head. Vermond fled, but was apprehended in Rue Saint-Denis. Two days later, Margot, dressed in mourning clothes, sat in a window of the *hôtel* and watched Vermond mount a scaffold constructed at the *hôtel*'s entrance, the very spot where the crime took place. Before the blade fell the condemned man was asked to make an "honorable amend" to the Queen. Vermond refused.

In a rage, Margot cried from her window, "Kill him, kill him!" And the blade fell. In grief over the loss of her Adonis, Queen Margot fled the Hôtel de Sens and moved to the Left Bank where she built a large mansion on Rue de Seine.

Look carefully at the facade of the Hôtel de Sens and you will find a cannon ball lodged in the stone, a reminder of the insurrection of 1830. The *hôtel* was bought by the city in 1911. Renovation was begun in 1936, but stopped during the war and then completed in 1955.

► Hôtel de Sens today.

▼◄ Hôtel de Sens courtyard, before and after. A comparison of the two photos shows the many liberties that were taken in the restoration. Note the different windows in each photo.

▲ Rue du Figuier. All the houses on this street were demolished in the 1930s and 1940s. Note the 15th-century niche placed on the corner of the building on the far right.

► Same view today. The building on the right dates from 1931.

► Rue du Figuier looking towards the Seine. Compare this to the photo on the opposite page. Same street, opposite direction.

◄◄ Rue du Figuier looking towards the Seine. Wider and with newer buildings. (photo, C. Olson)

◄ Medieval well that stood at 5 Rue du Figuier.

14 Rue du Fauconnier

Walk down this street to number 11.

▲ Rue du Fauconnier in 1913, still intact and long before demolition. Number 11 is the second building from the left. (photo, Pottier)

Rue du Fauconnier is recorded as early as 1265 and derives its name from the residence of the royal falconer that stood on this street. The building at number 11 dates from the 17th century and with its handsome facade, fine wrought iron balconies, and stunning carved wooden door, is nothing less than a youth hostel, one of three in this neighborhood, home to the Maison International de la Jeunesse et des Etudiants. It is worth entering to see the interior. In the aerial view opposite, taken during the demolitions of the 1940s, this building is in yellow.

▲ Rue du Fauconnier in December 1956, after the demolitions. Only number 11 is left standing. On the right is a new apartment building.

▲ 11 Rue du Fauconnier, today a youth hostel.

▲ Aerial view, circa 1940s, of much of this walk. In blue, large areas being cleared of buildings. In orange, buildings constructed in the 1930s. In green, buildings demolished later, in the 1950s. In yellow, 11 Rue du Fauconnier. (photo, Henrard)

⑮ Rue Charlemagne and Rue du Prévôt

At the end of Rue du Fauconnier, go left into Rue Charlemagne.

▲ Rue Charlemagne towards Rue du Figuier, circa 1940. The portion of building in blue matches the bottom photo on the facing page. Notice the street is deserted, the shops are closed. This was the Jewish quarter during the German occupation.

▼ Same view today.

The building at 16 Rue Charlemagne dates from 1892 and stands on the site of the Hôtel du Prévôt, constructed in the 15th and 16th centuries. The facade of today's building, ever so plain, was originally covered with embellishment more in keeping with the period, but was denuded in the 1950s when the owner wanted a look reflecting the streamlined aesthetic of the day. Little did he know how poorly this would age.

The Hôtel du Prévôt derived its name from Hughes Aubriot, Provost of Paris in 1367. The original structure was added onto and redesigned through the centuries as it changed hands. In 1516, the *hôtel* was divided in two with entrances on both Rue Charlemagne and around the corner on Rue du Prévôt. Among its many beautiful architectural details was a winding stone staircase within an octagonal tower dating back to Henri IV. The courtyard facade on the Rue Charlemagne side dated from the late Renaissance.

Demolition of the *hôtel* began in 1891 and is another example of a ruinous policy of urbanism in the quarter. The photo of the worker posing with his pickax on the facing page is as sad as photos of big game hunters posing with their rifle, great elephants lying dead at their feet. It is recommended that the reader *not* walk down Rue du Prévôt to see what was built on that side. It will make you ill. Do notice at the corner the old street name, Rue Percée, chiseled in the side of the building. That was the name of this tiny passageway from the 13th century until 1877 when it received its present name.

► Courtyard of Hôtel du Prévôt, circa 1900. (photo, Seeberger)

▼ 16 Rue Charlemagne today.

◄ Hôtel du Prévôt. The courtyard is in demolition. The building in blue is on Rue Charlemagne and is visible on the preceding page.

⑯ Rue Charlemagne and Rue du Figuier

Walk to the corner of these two streets.

▶ This building at the corner of Rue Charlemagne (on left) and Rue du Figuier (on right) is visible on p. 160. Notice the paper on the shutters of the second-floor windows to insulate against the cold.

▲ Same view today.

▲ Rue Charlemagne after demolition of the south side in 1946. Across the street is 16 Rue Charlemagne. To find the point of view of this photo, walk down Rue du Figuier a few steps. Imagine looking through the present building towards 16 Rue Charlemagne. The arched doorway on the left is the same arch pictured at the end of the street in the photo on p. 160.

▶ 16 Rue Charlemagne.

◀▲ 20 Rue Charlemagne, before and after restoration. The corner building was saved from demolition. The building to the left was less fortunate.

▶▼ 24 Rue Charlemagne, before and after restoration. It is most unusual that nothing was built in place of the corner building that was torn down.

⑰ **Rue de Fourcy**

Follow Rue Charlemagne to the corner of Rue de Fourcy.

▶ Rue de Fourcy, 1942. The building on the right with the metallic overhang matches the building on the left in the photo at the bottom of p. 163.

▼ Same view today. The first two buildings on the right were torn down.

◀ This building at 6 Rue de Fourcy has now become the first building on the street. Match the arch with the photo on the left. Notice the storefronts have been eliminated.

▶ 3 Rue de Fourcy, demolished in the 1960s. The Pétain government posters announce a coming draft. This was of no concern to Roman Rembelski, whose perfume/stationery store has been closed and boarded up.

▲ Same view. A home for the aged stands here today. (photo, M. Olson)

▼ 5 Rue de Fourcy. The walls are covered with posters of Pétain's government of collaboration.

◀ Same view. Today the Maison Européenne de la Photographie. (photo, M. Olson)

⑱ Rue des Nonnains-d'Hyères

Walk down Rue des Nonnains-d'Hyères towards the Seine.

▲ Maison du Châteaux Frileux, built in 1755 on the corner of Rue Charlemagne and Rue des Nonnains-d'Hyères, 1913. The ground floor still housed shops. Note the wraparound sign on the corner of the building, typical of 19th-century Paris.

◄ Maison du Châteaux Frileux during restoration in 1947–48. Three bays have been added along the side of Rue des Nonnains-d'Hyères.

► View of Maison du Châteaux Frileux today.

▲ Kitty-corner from the Maison du Châteaux Frileux on the Rue de Jouy is this reproduction of a 17th-century sign of a knife sharpener. See the lower photo on p. 169, where the original sign is visible on the corner building. The original is at the Musée Carnavalet.

▼ Rue des Nonnains-d'Hyères looking north before street widening in 1942–43. The building in blue is the Maison du Châteaux Frileux. The second building on the right still stands. The storefront has been eliminated.

▼ Same view today. The street, greatly widened, is barely recognizable.

▲ Rue des Nonnains-d'Hyères looking towards the Seine in 1958. All the buildings seen here on Quai des Célestins are in demolition. As the height of absurdity the building on the right corner had just undergone an extensive renovation.

▲ Same view today of Rue des Nonnains-d'Hyères.

⑲ Rue de l'Hôtel de Ville

Follow Rue des Nonnains-d'Hyères to Rue de l'Hôtel de Ville.

▲ Rue de l'Hôtel de Ville, circa 1900. The wall on the left encloses the garden of the Hôtel de Sens.

▲ Same view today. The Hôtel de Sens has been restored and the garden wall taken down. On the right, new construction. The street is no wider than before.

▶ This row of buildings on Quai des Célestins was torn down in 1958, though not because they were irretrievably lost to decay (the building on the corner had just been entirely renovated), but in order to provide a better view of the Hôtel de Sens. This followed an old concept in urban planning that sought to isolate monuments from their surroundings in order to better show them off. The original plan was to convert this vacated land into a garden. No sooner had the buildings been torn down than this decision was reversed and the present buildings were constructed. The oft-used reason for demolishing old buildings in order to widen streets was not even applied here. Rue de l'Hôtel de Ville today is as narrow as it was in medieval times.

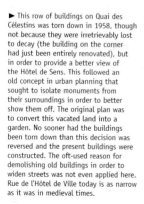

► The illustration shows the absurdity of isolating the Hôtel de Sens. Torn from its historical context, standing in the middle of what writer Albert Mousset aptly called an "administrative bombardment," the building loses all meaning. Context is everything. Bordered by a ridiculously wide street, the *hôtel* looks like stage décor, a palace of kitsch straight out of Las Vegas. Minister of Culture André Malraux said it well in 1962: "In architecture, an isolated masterpiece risks becoming a dead masterpiece." (*L'Illustration*, May 1938; ©BHVP/Negative Leyris)

► Rue de l'Hôtel de Ville at the corner of Rue des Nonnains-d'Hyères in 1942. This is the north side of the street. On the corner above the door is the sculpted sign of the knife sharpener, also visible in the photo below.

► Same corner as above seen from Rue des Nonnains-d'Hyères. The knife-sharpening sign is clearly recognizable. Everything here was demolished. (photo, Moreau Frères)

▲ Same view as photo to right. In the distance is the Cité Internationale des Arts.

㉒ Quai de l'Hôtel de Ville

Cross the street and look at the Cité Internationale des Arts.

For nearly six hundred years, Rue de l'Hôtel de Ville was called Rue de la Mortellerie. In 1832 a cholera epidemic struck Paris, killing nineteen thousand people. Three hundred died on this street alone. The surviving residents demanded that the name be changed because they did not want a street name that contained the word *mort*—death.

The Hôtel d'Aumont, now set back from the street behind a steel fence, dates from 1644 and was built from plans by Le Vau, one of the principal architects of Versailles. Later additions were carried out by Mansart. One of the most notable events to take place here was a lavish celebration held on December 4, 1771, that marked the signing of a marriage contract between scientist Antoine Lavoisier and Marie-Anne Pierette Paulze. Lavoisier, one of the founders of modern chemistry, was then twenty-eight years old and already a member of the Academy of Sciences. In 1794, during the Revolution, he was condemned to the guillotine. He pleaded to live a few more days in order to finish experiments he was working on, but was denied.

During the Revolution the Hôtel d'Aumont was confiscated by the state and for years passed between private and public hands, becoming in 1802 a town hall for what was then the 9th arrondissement of Paris, and later a public school, the Lycée Charlemagne.

In 1859 the *hôtel* was bought by the city and turned

▲ These buildings were torn down in 1942. On the extreme right is the corner building with the sign of the knife sharpener. (photo, Marcel Bovis; ©Ministère de la Culture/France)

▼ Same view today. In the distance, the Hôtel d'Aumont.

into offices for the Pharmacie Centrale de France. This greatly degraded the site, as the garden was covered over with what the French aptly call "parasite structures," including various sheds and hangars. The interior of the *hôtel* was converted to office space. The ensuing dismemberment of rooms coupled with a low level of maintenance sent the condition of the hôtel into a deteriorating spiral.

In 1931, the corporation that owned the Pharmacie offered to sell the *hôtel* to the city, but the offer was turned down. With news that the corporation would then tear the *hôtel* down, divide the property into lots, and sell them off individually, the city relented, and in 1936 purchased the site. It was in a terrible state of decay. For years the building stood empty and unprotected as thieves had scavenged everything that could be removed, and sections of the 17th-century floor were torn up by city workers to fuel their wood-burning stoves. Restoration was finally carried out between 1960 and 1963.

For some time the idea was floated of incorporating the *hôtel* into the Cité Internationale de Arts, but this went nowhere. Today the *hôtel* houses the

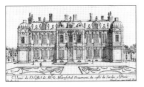

▲ Hôtel d'Aumont in the 17th century. (engraving, Israël Sylvestre; Musée Carnavalet, ©PMVP/Negative Joffre)

◀ Hôtel d'Aumont, circa 1940, in a state of abandon that went on for twenty more years.

▶ Hôtel d'Aumont after restoration, seen from Rue de l'Hôtel de Ville.

◀ This long row of buildings on Quai de l'Hôtel de Ville was demolished in 1941 to open a small, innocuous garden. A poor trade.

▲ Paul Tournon, one of the principal architects of the Cité Internationale des Arts and in charge of restoration for the Hôtel d'Aumont is seen here with a model for the Cité. What a difference between his plan and the final result.

Administrative Tribunal for the Department of the Seine.

It is most unfortunate that the Hôtel d'Aumont sits in such an unpleasant surrounding. Its well-tended garden is invisible and inaccessible to the public, while the whole is sequestered behind an utterly unattractive steel fence. The site is further disfigured by the entrance to the underground parking garage on the Rue Nonnains-d'Hyères side.

▲ Cité Internationale des Arts at the corner of Quai de l'Hôtel de Ville and the corner of Rue Geoffroy l'Asnier.

㉑ Rue Geoffroy l'Asnier

Follow Rue de l'Hôtel de Ville to Rue Geoffroy l'Asnier and go right.

The building on the corner, 50 Rue de l'Hôtel de Ville and 5–7 Rue Geoffroy l'Asnier, like many others in the quarter, had been approved for demolition but was saved by the l'Association Pour la Sauvegarde et Mise en Valeur du Paris Historique and restored in 1971. Today it serves as part of the Cité Internationale des Arts. Notice the absence of storefronts on the left side of the street after demolition and rebuilding. Another case of The Great Blight of Dullness. In the 18th century, a young Danton, having just arrived in Paris, stayed at the Auberge du Cheval Noir, located on this street.

▲ Rue Geoffroy l'Asnier in 1942. With the exception of the last building, a school, everything on the left side of the street was torn down around 1960.

▲ 12 Rue Geoffroy l'Asnier, demolished.

► Rue Geoffroy l'Asnier in its modern state of lethargy.

▶ 19 Rue Geoffroy l'Asnier in April 1942. Only the school at the far end of the street remains today. The buildings in the foreground were demolished in 1943. In their place stands the Memorial to the Unknown Jewish Martyr, built in 1956 and enlarged in 1992.

▲ Hôtel de Châlons Luxembourg at 26 Rue Geoffroy l'Asnier. Built in 1625–26 and restored in 1990. The large sculpted entryway is a masterpiece of 17th-century architecture. In this vintage photo, notice the shops that were eliminated during the restoration. In a misguided plan for urban renewal in the 1930s, the hotel was to be disassembled stone by stone and reassembled in Rue François-Miron. (photo, Atget)

▶ Hôtel de Châlons Luxembourg today.

22 Allée des Justes

Take Allée des Justes to Rue du Pont Louis-Philippe. Turn left and walk towards the Seine.

The Allée des Justes extends only one block to Rue du Pont Louis-Philippe. For over six hundred years this short street was known as Rue Grenier sur l'Eau. It received its present name in the spring of 2001 in homage to the "Just Ones" who helped save Jews during the occupation.

Rue du Pont Louis-Philippe was cut through in 1833 in order to continue Rue Vieille du Temple to the Seine and was named after the bridge that was built on the Seine that same year. The creation of this street cut Rue Grenier sur l'Eau in half. All that remains today is the short section in front of you.

▶ Rue Grenier sur l'Eau in June 1956.

▶ Same view today. The street was renamed Allée des Justes in 2001.

▲ Rue Grenier sur l'Eau between Rue du
Pont Louis-Philippe and Rue des Barres,
July 1899. The building on the right
dates from 1530 and was torn down for
useless street widening in 1959.
(photo, Atget)

► Same view today.

㉓ Rue du Pont Louis-Philippe

Cross the street and stand near the bridge to look back towards Rue des Barres and Rue du Pont Louis-Philippe.

111. PARIS — Place du Pont Louis-Philippe   E. L. D.

▲ This photo of Rue du Pont Louis-Philippe was taken from the bridge of the same name, circa 1900. The first building on the right with the sidewalk café was demolished. It is part of the same row of buildings pictured on p. 171, third photo from top. The building in blue still stands on Rue de l'Hôtel de Ville. Compare to photo below.

▶ Same view today.

▲ View of Rue du Pont Louis-Philippe on the right and Rue des Barres on the left.

▲ Same view today. Notice the buildings on the corner of Rue des Barres have been torn down.

► Corner of Rue des Barres and Rue de l'Hôtel de Ville. All the buildings on the left were torn down. Note the restaurant sign with two pigeons over the door.

4.36

Vieux Paris

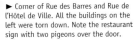

▲ The two pigeons are still in place over the door of this restaurant. Match with the photo on right.

La Rue des Barres
(anciennement rue du Chevet St-Gervais)
A l'angle de la rue de l'Hôtel-de-Ville, vieille enseigne " Les deux Pigeons"

㉔ **Rue des Barres**

Cross the street and walk to Rue des Barres, which runs parallel to Rue du Pont Louis-Philippe.

▲ Corner of Rue des Barres (on right) and Rue de l'Hôtel de Ville (on left). These buildings were demolished in 1945. (photo, Cayeux)

▲ Same corner in June 1953. The concept of pedestrian streets was not yet in vogue and Rue des Barres was still open to automobiles. Match the building on the right with the large photo on p. 177.

▼ A view from the bell tower of the Church of Saint-Gervais. Below, demolition in Rue des Barres and Rue de l'Hôtel de Ville. Colored blue, the site of the building in the picture above, left.

In the early 15th century, on the site of 2–10 Rue des Barres, stood the Hôtel des Barres, built in 1250. In 1417 Louis de Boisredon, a resident of the *hôtel*, became lover to the wife of the mad King Charles VI. When the king learned that he had been cuckolded he had the malfactor sewn up tight in a cloth sack and thrown into the Seine. On the sack was written, "Let the King's justice be done."

In the 17th century, the Hôtel des Barres was demolished and replaced by the Hôtel de Charny. During the Revolution, Robespierre was arrested in a bloody confrontation at Hôtel de Ville, and his younger brother was gravely injured when he tried to escape from a second-story window and fell to the ground. He was arrested and carried on a chair down Rue des Barres to the Hôtel de Charny. The next day they were both guillotined.

Walk up the street to the Church of Saint-Gervais. Rue des Barres is one of the oldest inhabited places on the Right Bank. In the first centuries after Christ this area was a marshland dotted with small stony mounds settled by populations of Gallo-Roman fisherman and boatmen. You are standing on one of those mounds. Notice the slightly higher elevation of the Rue des Barres.

Around 300 AD the inhabitants of this mound created a cemetery on its north side. In the 6th century the Christians built a funeral chapel on that spot dedicated to the Christian martyrs Gervais and Protais. That chapel was the origin of today's church, construction of which was begun in 1494. The first stone of today's facade was placed in 1616.

During the Revolution, an attempt to destroy the

▲ Corner of Rue des Barres and Rue Grenier sur l'Eau. The building on the left dates from 1530 and was torn down in 1959. The girls are standing in front of a 14th-century building, today a youth hostel.

◀ Same view today.

◀ Rue des Barres, circa 1940. (photo, Cayeaux)

church with explosives failed. Desacralized, it was then converted into the Temple of Youth. The church was restored in the 1820s and 1830s by Baltard, architect of the old Les Halles. More recently it was a scene of disaster. On Good Friday, 1918, the Germans fired a shell from Big Bertha and made a direct hit on the church. Scores of worshipers were killed and the second and third bays of the nave were destroyed.

▲ Rue des Barres, today a pedestrian street. Note the building at the end of the street and match it with the same in the photo on p. 177. Windows have been added, plus an additional floor.

25 Place Baudoyer

Follow Rue des Barres to Rue François-Miron.

▲ This space, formerly the site of the ancient cemetery of the Church of Saint-Gervais, became a courtyard, covered over to provide work space for neighborhood artisans.

▲ Same site after *curetage* carried out by Albert Laprade. (Commission du Vieux Paris)

At the corner, look to your left, to the long stairway and the row of buildings fronting Place Baudoyer. Behind these buildings is a small garden, pictured above. This is the location of the cemetery dating back to Roman times, mentioned earlier. The cemetery grew in size and at one point extended out to Place Baudoyer. In 1375 a wall was built along Rue François-Miron, on the site of today's buildings, to enclose the cemetery. Vendors settled along this wall selling fish, meat, and fruit, and remained here until 1475 when the wall was torn down and the first houses were built. The present houses, known as the Elm houses because of the elm motif on the balconies, were constructed during the reign of Louis XV, between 1733 and 1737.

In 1941, the condition of these houses was judged so deplorable that the city planned to demolish them. Architect Albert Laprade argued vigorously for their restoration and won the city over. Restoration took place between 1943 and 1946.

A more radical plan than tearing down these houses was conceived by Haussmann in 1868. He wanted to cut a new street between Place Baudoyer and Quai des Célestins near the Hôtel de Sens. Ninety-eight buildings would have been demolished had this plan been carried out.

▲ View from Place Baudoyer of the Elm houses on the right dating from 1733–37. (photo, Cayeux)

▲ The site after restoration.

▲ Corner of Rue des Barres and Rue François-Miron. These buildings date from 1665, and were part of the mindless demolition carried out in this quarter in 1958.

▲ Same view today. The present buildings date from 1960.

► Haussmann's project for creating a new thoroughfare, in red, from Place Baudoyer to Quai des Célestins. The Church of Saint-Gervais is in yellow; Rue des Barres, in green; Rue des Nonnains-d'Hyères, in blue. (1868)

㉖ Rue François-Miron

Follow Rue François-Miron eastward in the direction of traffic.

▲ 11, 13 Rue François-Miron before restoration. (l'Association pour la Sauvegarde et la Mise en Valeur du Paris Historique)

▲ Now more medieval than ever, these houses were zealously restored in 1966–67. That they date from the 15th century as claimed may be true, but their restoration involved a good dose of fantasy as well. Note the change in roofline of the building on the left. The stone facade on the ground floor level is not made of solid block but only a thin layer of stone facing. The position of the windows on both buildings has been altered.

For several hundred years this narrow street was part of a grand entry into Paris leading directly to the palace of the Louvre. It was only eclipsed by Haussmann's completion of Rue de Rivoli, begun by Napoléon I in the early 1800s.

◄ 42 Rue François-Miron. This building was designed by architect Pierre de Vigny (1742), who also designed the Cour du Dragon (see p. 18). Despite its elegance, this building was threatened with demolition in 1939.

◄ 44–46 Rue François-Miron. This building, Maison d'Ourscamp, dates from 1585 and was constructed on foundations of a much older building dating back to 1255. The 13th-century cellar, still gloriously intact, is well worth the visit. This photo shows the terrible state of the building in the early 1960s. City bureaucrats judged it lost and proceeded towards demolition. It stands today only because of the tenacity of the local neighborhood preservation organization l'Association pour la Sauvegarde et Mise en Valeur du Paris Historique. With volunteer labor working weekends for over twenty years, they restored the building to its former beauty. (Association pour la Sauvegarde et la Mise en Valeur du Paris Historique)

▶ The Maison d'Ourscamp is built over a cellar with vaulted ceilings dating from 1255. (photo, M. Turin)

▲ 44–46 Rue François-Miron after restoration. Today the building houses offices of l'Association pour la Sauvegarde et Mise en Valeur du Paris Historique.

㉗ Rue de Jouy

Walk to the corner of Rue François-Miron and Rue Tiron. Go left about fifty feet and turn around. Then cross Rue François-Miron and walk down Rue de Jouy about 50 yards.

▲ These buildings at the corner of Rue de Jouy and Rue François-Miron were torn down in 1945. The building with the large sign dated from the era of Louis XIII (late 16th, early 17th century). Note Impasse Guepine between the third and fourth building from the left. Compare this to next page. (photo, Atget)

◄ Same view today. These buildings were constructed in 1992.

► Rue de Jouy towards Rue
François-Miron. At the corner on the
right is Impasse Guepine. Everything
here was demolished.

▼ Same view today. The buildings
date from 1992.

◄ Impasse Guepine during the
German occupation. A poster on the
building advertises an anti-Semitic
exhibition, "France and the Jew."
(photo, Cayeaux)

28 From Rue de Jouy to Saint-Paul

Continue on Rue François-Miron to the middle of the next block and the Hôtel de Beauvais.

▶ Hôtel de Beauvais. Designed by architect Antoine Le Pautre. Commissioned by Pierre Beauvais and his wife, Catherine Bellier. Built between 1655 and 1660. Madame de Beauvais was first chambermaid to Louis XIV's mother, Anne of Austria. The two women had a most intimate connection. Not only did Beauvais administer the Queen Mother her colonics, she deflowered the queen's sixteen-year-old son, Louis. Anne was overjoyed at the news. Her husband, Louis XIII, suffered from sexual dysfunction—it took the couple twenty-two years to conceive—and Anne was most apprehensive for her son. It being the fashion at court to imitate the king, Catherine de Beauvais' sexual favors became much in demand. She counted among her lovers the most pious Archbishop of Sens, Henri-Louis de Gondrin.

On August 26, 1660, Louis XIV and his wife, Marie Thérèse, made a triumphal entry into Paris passing along Rue Saint-Antoine and Rue François-Miron. Louis rode a chestnut mare covered in a brocade of silver and precious stones. Marie Thérèse rode in a superb carriage covered in gold and silver and pulled by six pearl gray horses. On their route, the royal procession stopped in front of the Hôtel de Beauvais to salute the Queen Mother standing on a richly decorated balcony, the same balcony before you. Among the coterie at her side was Louis's aunt, Henrietta Maria, widow of England's King Charles I, who only months earlier had been beheaded by Oliver Cromwell during the English Revolution.

As Catherine de Beauvais grew older she also grew large and unattractive. Never losing her strong sexual desire, however, it was she who had to pay for sexual favors. After her husband's death in 1674 she found herself saddled with huge debt that reduced her to a pauper. In the end she lived destitute at the Hôtel de Beauvais as a simple renter.

In 1763 the *hôtel* came into the possession of the Bavarian ambassador, who received a visit that year from Mr. Leopold Mozart and his wife and children. Among them little Wolfgang, age seven. The young prodigy performed for the royal family at Versailles and gave an organ recital in the chapel there. The *hôtel* stood in a terrible state for years awaiting restoration. This was finally completed in 2003. Today it contains offices for a city agency and is unfortunately inaccessible to the public.

▲ Hôtel de Beauvais on Rue François-Miron. (from *Les Vieux Hôtels de Paris*, 10ᵉ série, Contet & Vacqiuer; ©BHVP/Negative Leyris)

▲◀ Courtyard of the Hôtel de Beauvais. For some time turned over for use as a theater. (from *Les Vieux Hôtels de Paris*, 10ᵉ série, Contet & Vacquier; ©BHVP/Negative Leyris)

▲ Hôtel Hénault de Cantobre at 82
Rue François-Miron. Built in 1706. This
is certainly one of the most beautiful
facades anywhere in Paris. Today this
building houses the Maison Européenne
de la Photographie, with an entrance on
Rue de Fourcy. The building underwent
extensive restoration in 1993 (but was
almost demolished along with others on
the street in the 1930s).

▲ Hôtel de Beauvais in the 17th century.

▶ Rue François-Miron in June 1970.
Note the Hôtel Hénault de Cantobre
before restoration, second building
from left. The corner building still
stands except for the store, which was
eliminated to build an arcade on Rue
de Fourcy.

㉙ Saint-Paul

At the end of Rue François-Miron, walk over to the island near the Métro entrance.

▲ 133 Rue Saint-Antoine around 1900. This building, housing a cafe to this day, was constructed in 1626. Note the sculptures of chimeras supporting the balcony that dates from 1728, hence the name of today's café, Café Chimeres. Note also the number 88 on either side of the archway. This was the number of the building before Haussmann opened the Rue de Rivoli here, thus changing the name of this street from Rue Saint-Antoine to Rue Francois Miron.

Now that you have completed this walk it is time to tell the real story of what you have seen. You have just walked through the famous *îlot* (sector) 16, bound on the north by Rues François-Miron and Saint-Antoine, on the east by Rue Saint-Paul, on the south by Quai des Célestins, and on the west by Rue de Brosse next to the Church of Saint-Gervais.

In March 1936, the city put forth a plan to raze the entire *îlot* 16 to the ground. Consider that. Everything in this sector, all the buildings you saw, with the exception of a few of the most historical such as the Hôtel de Sens, the Church of Saint-Gervais, and the Church of Saint-Paul, were

to be demolished. What would account for such extreme action?

In 1894 the Prefecture of the Seine undertook an inspection of all 79,982 buildings in Paris in order to determine their degree of hygiene. Buildings clustered together in the same neighborhood with a high mortality rate from tuberculosis were judged "contaminated" and tagged *îlot insalubre*—a block of unhealthy dwellings to be demolished.

What the study did not recognize was the condition of poverty that led to this unhealthy living environment. Tuberculosis is a highly contagious disease that requires early detection and quarantine. Unlike the wealthy, who could

afford a visit to the doctor at the earliest sign of symptoms, the poor could not. Too often the disease was well advanced before it was caught, and in the meantime others had been infected too. But the disease, it was thought, was in the stones.

By 1921, seventeen *îlots insalubres* had been identified. The order of the list was based on the severity of the problem. Number one on the list was the *îlot* Beaubourg on the Right Bank, demolished in the 1930s and today the site of the Centre Pompidou. By 1936, little else had been accomplished. Then suddenly *îlot* 16 was pushed to the top of the list. Parisians were slow to understand the reason why. The Hôtel de Ville sits on the western edge of *îlot* 16. With city agencies spread all over Paris in cramped, antiquated quarters, city planners were seduced by the idea of demolishing this quarter and building a complex of new, modern office buildings in order to gather all the city agencies into one area. An initiative to grapple with a genuine health problem had been thrown off course.

In March of that year the full scope of the city's plans were made public in an exhibition held at l'Hôtel de Ville. Parisians found the three-dimensional models of an obliterated Paris shocking. Vigorous protest derailed the project and sent the urbanists back to the drawing boards.

Over the next several years plans for *îlot* 16 went through revision after revision, each advocating one form or another of major demolition. One example of these diabolical plans, conceived in 1939 by architects André Hilt and Henri Bodecher, shows the full scope of this madness. Hilt was unequivocal in pushing forward his vision, writing "There are cases when excessive conservation of old buildings is a crime against society." The excessive conservation Hilt was against included preserving the Hôtel d'Aumont, Hôtel Hénault de Cantobre, Hôtel Seguier (Café Chimeres), and the 12th-century wall of Philippe-Auguste. In Hilt's plan, all these were to be destroyed. Hilt drove home his rationale further. "Let us not forget," he wrote, "that these buildings are the cause of an excessively high mortality rate, and because of this the

▲ Saint-Paul bombed by the Germans in World War I. The building colored blue was later torn down for the widening of Rue Geoffroy l'Asnier.

morality of their proprietors is questionable." Morality?

Where was the morality of pushing *îlot* 16 to the top of the list while thousands of Parisians lived in far more threatening circumstances? Where was the morality of extending *îlot* 16 west beyond the areas judged contaminated, in order to include buildings around Saint-Gervais that had never been called into question medically? Anyone curious to see what Hilt's nightmarish vision would have produced need only go to Boulevard Morland, a short street on the Seine, to see the Centre Morland built in 1971.

In 1941 when it looked like *îlot* 16 was a lost cause, a great defender of historic Paris, Maurice Raval, had an idea: Assemble a petition arguing for the preservation of the *îlot* signed by leading artists and intellectuals and present this petition to Marshal Pétain. The idea worked. Pétain had a soft spot for old Paris and quashed plans for major demolition. This was a turning point.

For the first time the city administration acknowledged the historic value of the *îlot* and stated a desire to maintain its 17th-century character.

But how are public works projects on such a scale to be carried out while the buildings in question are still inhabited? In German-occupied Paris, the answer was easy. Anti-semitism did not create *îlot* 16, but during these war years it did help facilitate the aims of those wishing to demolish the area.

All properties in *îlot* 16 were confiscated by the Department of Health and all inhabitants were evicted. Renters had thirty days to vacate. Businesses were to leave the premises. Affected were 10,515 people, 4,898 households, and 419 businesses. It wasn't bad enough that the Jewish population lived in fear of being shipped off to concentration camps. Now in the dead of winter and with nowhere to go (Jews were forbidden to leave Paris), they were forced to move. A request made during the

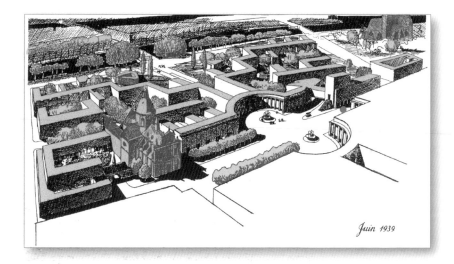

Juin 1939

▲ Project put forth in 1939 for the massive demolition of the *îlot* 16 by André Hilt, winner of the Grand Prix de Rome, and Henri Bodecher. In the foreground is Rue Saint-Antoine. Monuments to be saved are in blue; Church of Saint-Paul Saint-Louis, Hotel de Sens, Church of Saint-Gervais. Red point indicates final stop on this walk at Métro Saint-Paul. (Color added by the author.)

winter of 1942 to delay the expulsions was refused on grounds that it would "create a precedent." The infamous roundups in which thousands of Jews were shipped off to the death camps left hundreds of apartments empty, thus serving city bureaucrats well. Shortly after the roundup known as the Rafle du Vel d'Hiv in July 1942, Albert Laprade wrote, "All of a sudden the quarter was empty, no more men, women or children. What happened to them? The apartments were empty. The broken doors were left open."

Standing empty, these same buildings were left to deteriorate in a policy of deliberate neglect. Pillaging became common

and everything sellable was carted off. Those in city government who were obliged to follow Pétain's decree of conservation, yet who harbored a deep abhorrence for the quarter, nursed hopes that if the buildings were left to deteriorate long enough they would eventually be torn down as a matter of public safety. In 1944, the Hôtel d'Aumont, long exposed to the elements, was "condemned" by the city. Fortunately, the architect Michel Roux-Spitz stepped in and saved it.

By war's end a huge bureaucracy that had been grinding on for years had taken a devastating toll in the quarter. In 1948, Alfred Mousset of the Commission of Old Paris remarked aptly

that *îlot* 16 had been "a victim of an administrative bombardment." The destruction continued on through the 1950s and 1960s. The aerial photo on p. 159 shows the extent of the demolition carried out.

How many Parisians today know of the countless dramas that were played out in this section of Paris? Given the powerful forces that tried to demolish the quarter it is tempting to say that it is a miracle that anything remains at all. In truth there were no miracles, only hard work carried out by people uninterested in edifying their egos in stone, and with no desire for personal or financial gain, motivated only by their love of this great city.

Epilogue

We would like to think that we live in a more enlightened era today and that the gross abuses that disfigured Paris in the past will not happen again. We would like to think that the mentality that conceived of Paris as only a convenience for the automobile, as shown with the plan of turning the quai along the Left Bank into a freeway mirroring the Right Bank, is extinct. We would like to think that the mentality that conceived of building a parking garage under the Place des Vosges with the entrance on the Place, an idea that would have thoroughly disfigured the Place, is extinct. We would like to think that we are beyond this. But this is an illusion.

In 1967, architect Pierre Dufau wrote, "In August 1944, General von Choltitz disobeyed his orders and did not blow up Paris. No one asked himself afterwards if we should not have shot this man ourselves because he deprived us of our only chance to, in good conscience, to renovate, therefore, to save our capital. Destruction is a necessity of renovation. We can demolish. We must demolish that which is definitely dead." (From *Paris, Biography of a Capital*, Pierre Pinon.) People such as Dufau appear as monstrous figures from a science fiction movie, perhaps *Night of the Living Dead*. They no longer think

or feel like humans. Their psychosis is of the most sophisticated order. They are cool, calm, articulate, and above all, relentlessly logical. Their arguments are well thought out, well presented. And the world they want to deliver us into is a nightmare.

Now we learn that the landmark in urban planning, the Malraux Law, is in danger. Since its creation in the early 1960s, the law's measures protecting the safeguarded sectors in Paris operated under the aegis of the Conseil d'Etat. This is no longer the case. Now these measures fall under the purview of a variety of different agencies, including ministries, commissions, and municipal councils. This weakens these safeguards and makes them vulnerable. There is no longer the necessary blanket prohibition against the demolition of buildings in these protected sectors; rather, this prohibition can be lifted for a building "given certain conditions" (*soumises à des*

◄ Place Dauphine. One wing was demolished by Haussmann. His plan to demolish the entire *place* was fortunately never carried out.

◄ Entry to Cour du Dragon. Demolished in 1958.

conditions speciales). There is the loophole! There is little chance that the Marais will disappear in an immense urban project like those that wiped out whole Paris neighborhoods in years past. The danger today, rather, is that the Marais and other safeguarded sectors in Paris will be nibbled to death building by building. Paris is never saved. It is always in the process of being saved.

I give the last word to Woody Allen. In 2000, Allen appeared before the New York City Landmarks Preservation Commission to oppose plans for an apartment building in his Upper East Side neighborhood. The commission had already rejected an earlier version of the project and was considering a scaled-down revision. Allen objected to the new design, saying "If, if, one was to take a, a, a genuine work of art, a painting, a, a Van Gogh for example, a, um, a vase with some sunflowers in it, and developers came along and said, 'Look, this has been great for years, but progress is progress, and we would like to add a half dozen sunflowers to this picture and we'll make them consistent with the sunflowers that are already in there, but, you know, we feel it would beautify and it's in the name of progress and development,' and they go before the equivalent of the landmarks commission but in the field of art and in the spirit of, of compromise, they say, 'Well, we won't give you six, we'll give you three sunflowers,' the, the, the point is obvious. The whole, the whole thing is ruined." Woody gets it.

Acknowledgments

This book is a product of my passion for Paris. It is a book that I had to write. There was never a proposal submitted in hopes of getting an advance that would enable me to carry out the research I needed to do. I have never been affiliated with a university or institution of higher learning. Thus the five years of research for this book were carried out with no grants or subsidies of any kind.

But there were individuals who helped me along my way. Firstly I would like to thank Marie de Thézy, whose book *Marville* began me on the journey that led to this book. The impressive portrait she assembled of pre-Haussmann Paris was both a revelation and an inspiration. Others who served as guides, who knew to ask me the right questions or provide information I was looking for at a crucial moment, were Alexandre Gady, Susan Griffin, Edith Sorel, and Odette Meyers. The support of Victoria Shoemaker, Kristin Leimkuhler, Carrie Olson, and Christine Lauer was most meaningful. Special gratitude to Donald Galfond, a man who I met only once, but whose interest in my work developed into a long email correspondence during which he generously gave of his time and erudition to iron out the many wrinkles of my manuscript.

Nothing would have been possible without the availability of the photographic archives in Paris, and to those who manage them I am indebted. Those who showed remarkable patience were Francoise Réynaud of the Musée Carnavalet, Antonella Casellato of the Pavillon de l'Arsenal, the people at the Photothèque des Musées de la Ville de Paris, and Gérard Leyris of the Bibliothèque Historique de la Ville de Paris.

And finally my gratitude to those who for years fought on the front lines to preserve historic Paris, people with vision and imagination without whom the Paris we love today would be much diminished. Among them: Lucien Lambeau, Georges Pillement, André Fermigier, Michel Raude, l'Association pour la Sauvegarde et Mise en Valeur du Paris Historique, Maurice Minost, and Pierre d'Espezel.

photo by Marvin Collins

I n 1963, Leonard Pitt left a career in advertising to study mime in Paris with Etienne Decroux. He returned to the United States seven years later, settling in Berkeley, California, where he directed a school of physical theatre until 1988. During that time, he traveled to Bali to study mask carving and mask theatre, which he performed with Balinese natives in temple and village festivals. In 1986, he co-founded Life on the Water, a San Francisco theatre presenting original work, and in 1991, created Eco-Rap, an environmental education program that combines ecology and rap music to inspire a new generation of environmentally conscious youth. *A Small Moment of Great Illumination,* his biography of 17th-century Anglo-Irish healer Valentine Greatrakes, is forthcoming and he is currently at work on a memoir of his years in Paris.

Visit his website at www.leonardpitt.com.